Contents

COVER PICTURES

Top: *A riot of multi-coloured onion domes
on the roof of St Basil's Cathedral in Moscow.*

Bottom: *Hungarians dress up to celebrate their
first free elections in 1990.*

Slav Lands of Splendour and Diversity

'Russia is not a state, but a world,' claims one of its old proverbs. Certainly, the most striking feature of the lands of Eastern Europe, combined with those of what used to be the Soviet Union, is the sheer scale and diversity of the region they encompass. Spanning two continents, Asia as well as Europe, it includes landscapes as different as the Alpine forests and pastures of the Carpathian Mountains sweeping across Poland, Romania and Slovakia, and the huge, nearly treeless plains of the Steppes spreading across the Eurasian landmass from the Ukraine to the Russian border with China. It ranges from the fertile vine, tobacco and rose-growing valleys of Bulgaria in the south to the frozen wastes of the Siberian tundra in the north.

The various Slav peoples that dominate much of the region impose a kind of unity, but their hold is by no means exclusive. Ethnic German communities survive in Romania and the Volga basin; the Balts of Lithuania, Latvia and Estonia cling fast to their own quite separate identities; the Romanians are fiercely proud of what they regard as their Latin roots, and the Hungarians of their distinctive Magyar heritage. Within the new Commonwealth of Independent States, there are the Oriental (and predominantly Muslim) peoples of Kazakhstan, Turkmenistan and Uzbekistan, not to mention such groups as the Tatars (Turkic-speaking descendants of some of the Steppes' original inhabitants) and the Cossacks, the battling Armenians and Azerbaidzhanis. In the circumstances, it is hardly surprising that the collapse of Soviet authority has been followed by such turmoil and uncertainty. Nor, on the other hand, is it surprising that out of this creative mix the region has produced so much to be proud of over the centuries: the architectural splendours of Prague, Cracow and St Petersburg; the impassioned music of Chopin, Liszt, Tchaikovsky, Dvorak and Bartok; the poetry of Pushkin and the novels of Turgenev, Tolstoy, Dostoyevsky and Kafka.

It is more than usually true to say of this huge slice of humanity that its present is shaped by its past. And in this, the Slavs have undoubtedly had a dominating influence. Originating in the eastern Carpathians around 2000 BC, they spread out during the succeeding centuries to the west, the south and the east: the so-called West Slavs became today's Poles, Czechs and Slovaks; the South Slavs populated much of the Balkans; the East Slavs colonised the rich black-earth plains of modern Russia, Belarus (Belorussia) and Ukraine.

Crucial to the Slavs' development as essentially European, westward-facing nations was their conversion to Christianity. Here, the Catholic and Orthodox churches both gained adherents. In AD 966, Mieszko I of Poland opted for the Christian religion in its Catholic form, thus creating the close ties between his country and Rome that have lasted to this day. The Czechs, Slovaks and many Ukrainians and Belorussians followed the same route. The Orthodox monks St Cyril and St Methodius, meanwhile, had left their mark farther east and south. In AD 863 they were despatched from Byzantium to the principality of Moravia

IN SEARCH OF RUSSIA AND EASTERN EUROPE

IN SEARCH

OF

RUSSIA

AND

EASTERN

EUROPE

Reader's
Digest

PUBLISHED BY THE READER'S DIGEST ASSOCIATION LIMITED

LONDON   NEW YORK   MONTREAL   SYDNEY   CAPE TOWN

Originally published in partwork form,
Des Pays et des Hommes,
by Librairie Larousse, Paris

A Reader's Digest selection

IN SEARCH OF RUSSIA AND EASTERN EUROPE

First English Edition Copyright © 1992
The Reader's Digest Association Limited, Berkeley Square House,
Berkeley Square, London W1X 6AB

Copyright © 1992
Reader's Digest Association Far East Limited
Philippines Copyright 1992
Reader's Digest Association Far East Limited

Originally published in French as a partwork,
Des Pays et des Hommes
Copyright © 1983, 1985
Librairie Larousse

Translated and edited by Toucan Books Limited, London
Translated and adapted by Andrew Kerr-Jarrett and Alex Martin

ISBN 0 276 42052 7

Printed by Printer Industria Gráfica S.A., Barcelona

on the banks of the Danube to preach the gospel and the Orthodox faith. Moravia, part of the modern Czech lands, would later revert to Catholicism, but not before Cyril had translated the Bible into Slavonic and devised a Slavic alphabet, based on Greek. He thus played a key part in the development of the Slavonic tongues as written languages, and his Cyrillic alphabet is still used by the Russians and Bulgarians.

The next turning point came a little over 100 years later. By the mid-10th century, a group of Slav tribes (though ruled by princes of Viking descent) had established themselves around Kiev in a principality known to the Byzantines as Rus. By 980, Grand Prince Vladimir I had successfully survived a period of dynastic conflict, and had consolidated his rule over a huge realm centred around Kiev and Novgorod and stretching as far as the Baltic. Later that decade, he became the first Christian ruler of the emerging Russian nation. The story has it that Vladimir was in two minds about which of the world's great faiths to adhere to. Islam he rejected out of hand because of its ban on alcohol, so he sent emissaries to assess the different branches of Christianity. They were unimpressed by much of what they saw: the Germans failed to appeal; the Bulgarians smelt bad. But they were dazzled by Byzantium: 'We knew not whether we were in heaven or earth,' they reported, 'for on earth there is no such vision nor beauty, and we do not know how to describe it; we know only that there, God dwells among men.' Sadly, the truth of the conversion probably has a more prosaic, self-interested element: Vladimir chose Orthodox Christianity in order to consolidate an alliance with the Byzantine emperor, whose sister he married. Either way, the effect was the same. The conversion was not merely a personal affair – Vladimir's subjects were expected to switch religions too. In Novgorod where some locals resisted, their idols were flung into the river Dnepr.

If Christianity in its different forms has been one determining influence on the peoples of Eastern Europe and Russia, the region's geography has been another. 'Think of an endless plain,' wrote the British author Maurice Baring when describing Russia in the early years of this century, 'a sheet of dazzling snow in winter, an ocean of golden corn in summer, a tract of brown earth in autumn, and now in the earliest days of spring an expanse of white melting snow with great patches of brown earth and sometimes green grass appearing . . .'

The great flat lands of the North European Plain and the Steppes have an undoubted beauty of their own, but equally they have a political disadvantage in that natural frontiers are, by the nature of things, extremely scarce. Communities would settle on the banks of great rivers such as the Volga and the Dnepr, but there was no natural landmark to indicate where the territory of one group might end and that of another begin. Strife among them was therefore common. One community would swallow up others by war or alliances; a great nation or even empire might emerge, with few natural limits to its expansion, but little in the way of a natural heartland, either. The expansion and contraction of these states could be dramatic. In the Middle Ages, Lithuania spread right across the plains of Central Europe and included much of the Ukraine; it is now a little smaller than Scotland. Russia expanded from Vladimir's already large realm, and under a series of ruthless princes (most notably Ivan the Terrible) shifted its centre north to Moscow. In 1712, Peter the Great founded his new capital St Petersburg as a 'window to the west'. Later tsars expanded their huge domains eastwards across Siberia to the Pacific and down into Central Asia. In this century, the Communist dictator Stalin fulfilled a long-held Russian ambition: in the post-Second World War Soviet empire in Central Europe, he created a vast buffer zone to protect the Russian heartland. The process of expansion has now slipped into reverse. The events of the 1980s and 90s have seen Russia stripped not only of its Warsaw Pact satellites, but even of much of the old Tsarist empire – which still, on the other hand, leaves it one of the largest and most populous nations on earth.

Farther west, meanwhile, the Czechs, Slovaks, Hungarians, Romanians, Bulgarians and others are facing the future from their homelands among the valleys, plains, hills and mountains of Central Europe and the Balkans. Even here, large multi-national empires (rather than relatively well-defined nation states, such as France, Britain or Spain) tended to be the norm – most notably the sprawling domains of the Habsburg empire, which fell apart in the aftermath of the First World War. Such empires left their heritage of problems. The borders of the new states created from them were inevitably somewhat arbitrary, leaving minority communities of ethnic Hungarians within Romania and Slovakia, of Turks within Bulgaria and so on. The prickly nationalisms of the various peoples all across Eastern Europe and the old Soviet Union, together with long-suppressed feuds and antipathies, are among the most alarming ingredients in the melting pot of the post-Cold War era.

The region, then, faces a period of considerable uncertainty. Moscow may have its McDonald's burger bar and other appurtenances of the long-envied Western lifestyle, but for most people food is, if anything, more scarce than in the old days. Not even the inspired leadership of the playwright and former president Vaclav Havel was sufficient to hold the Czechs and Slovaks together within one federal union. Market forces and the charismatic, if maverick, presidency of Lech Walesa, the former hero of the free trades union Solidarity, have not so far succeeded in bringing much political coherence to Poland. Even the small and relatively homogeneous Georgian nation in the Caucasus has its roots of strife, while poverty and chaos threaten to engulf some of the Islamic states of what used to be Soviet Central Asia. In most of these places, ordinary people can enjoy a renewed freedom after the years of tyranny and a new sense of pride in their nationhood. But in many cases fear remains: the fear of hunger as state systems adapt creakily to some form of capitalism, the fear of violence and death in the cause of some ancestral racial hatred, and always the nagging fear of a return to despotism.

But the picture is by no means all black. Perhaps the most heartening lesson to emerge from the years of tyranny is that of the sheer resilience of the peoples of Eastern Europe. Communist dictators came and went, but the people cracked their darkly satirical jokes and somehow survived. Catholicism withstood the anti-clerical tide in Poland; ancient festivals and folk customs continued throughout the region. Not even the gruesome Romanian tyrant Ceausescu was able to kill his countrymen's love of colour and festivity. In Central Asia, meanwhile, ancient cities such as Samarkand and Bukhara kept much of their exotic, Oriental appeal. Tyranny, racial hatred, environmental pollution, all have left their scars on the face of Eastern Europe and Russia, but still the people's spirit remains to an astonishing extent unquenched.

Commonwealth of Independent States

Flip through a picture book of the former Soviet Union and what do you see? Soldiers in Red Square, onion-domed churches, peasant women in white headscarves ... But now look further. The familiar images give way to something more exotic – Kyrgyz horsemen with hunting-eagles, turbanned water-melon sellers outside a Bukhara mosque, a pair of tigers padding through the Siberian snow. Today, as the 15 republics of the former USSR re-shape themselves for the future, it is worth discovering what a wealth of different peoples, landscapes and cultures they contain.

The Old Arbat, Moscow's
fashionable pedestrian
precinct, famous (since 1987)
for its portrait artists, street
theatres, cafés, ice-cream
stalls and shops.

The River Moskva, which
gave its name to the Russian
capital and supplies the city
with much of its water.
Through a network of canals,
the Moskva connects with the
Volga and thence to all of
European Russia's seas.

Previous page:
Red Square, with the
Cathedral of St Basil the
Blessed dominating the
skyline. In October 1990 a
service was held in the
cathedral for the first time
since 1924.

Citizens of the West

A landscape of apparently endless trees unfolds as you approach Moscow by car. Suddenly the city looms out of a gap in the forest, with blocks of flats towering over building sites to right and left. The traffic becomes heavier. You are entering the suburbs.

For a while the forest closes in again, then stops just short of the Motorway Ring, which marks the start of Moscow proper. Even when you are inside the city limits, trees keep reappearing – along the main avenues that converge on the Kremlin, or in the woods of Sokolniki Park. Moscow seems to have been carved out of the forest, an island in an ocean of green.

And yet the forest is threatened. It covers 40 per cent of the Moscow region and much of it is now designated as national parkland to protect it from the encroaching tower blocks of Moscow's satellite towns. This area was once the game reserve of the Tsars. Its wildlife is still rich and varied, with deer, elk, foxes and wolves, which can sometimes be seen prowling near the Motorway Ring.

Only by crossing the land in a train or car can one appreciate its sheer vastness. Six hundred miles separate Moscow from the Polish border. Railway and highway cross forest and plain with scarcely a bend and with hardly any rises or falls. Plantations of oak, maple, pine, spruce, hazel and birch succeed one another relentlessly – a reminder that nearly one-third of the former Soviet Union is covered in forests, which make up a fifth of the world's trees.

Getting to Moscow by train and ship from London takes just under fifty-four hours. You can do it on any day of the year, except Christmas Day or Boxing Day, from Liverpool Street Station. The route is London – Harwich – Hook of Holland – Rotterdam – Munster – Hanover – Berlin – Poznan – Warsaw – Brest – Minsk – Smolensk – Moscow. Despite encouraging knife-and-fork symbols on the timetable, and little black-and-white beds denoting sleeping berths, it has to be said that the full journey is something of an endurance test, and is likely to be actively enjoyed only by the most dedicated railway enthusiast.

A four-hour flight ends at Sheremetyevo, one of five Moscow airports. From the other four, aircraft are taking off night and day for the most distant corners of the former Soviet Union. The traffic never stops, since there is always a city in that immense land where it is day. Without the fleets of Ilyushins, Tupolevs and Yaks, modern life would be almost inconceivable. The Trans-Siberian Railway, for example, takes ten days to go from one end of Russia to the other.

The site of Moscow was first settled in Neolithic times. It was fortified in the mid-12th century and grew to prominence in the 200-year-long wars with the Mongols which began in 1236. By the end of the 15th century Moscow was the capital of the expanding state of Russia, and the city spread outwards from the Kremlin fortress to include monasteries, palaces and artisans' quarters. Trade, particularly in furs, flourished, as did cultural life with the first printing press

introduced in 1533 and the founding of a university in 1687. In 1712 Peter the Great moved his capital to the newly-built city of St Petersburg, but Moscow's commercial and cultural life continued to thrive, and many new buildings, including several textile factories, appeared in the 18th century. In 1812 Napoleon occupied the city but was forced to abandon it after fire destroyed two-thirds of the buildings. Reconstruction began soon after, and Moscow recovered its economic vigour, stimulated by a new stock exchange (1837) and the first railway (1851), which encouraged large numbers of peasants to move to the city for work. In the 1890s the first heavy industries were developed on the outskirts, and between 1835 and 1915 the population rose from 336,000 to almost 2 million. In 1918,

Moscow's metro, built in the 1930s, has spacious halls and concourses and lavish decoration. Trains run every three minutes at normal times, more frequently in the rush hour.

The silver birch, beryoza, *the Russians' favourite tree. It is found right across the country, stunted in the north, majestic and soaring in the forests of the centre. Its wood is still a basic material of everyday life. Birch twigs are used for a stimulating 'whip' before a sauna.*

The hourly changing of the guard at the Lenin Mausoleum in Moscow. Nowadays, it is foreign tourists rather than Russians who visit the mausoleum.

following the Bolshevik revolution, Moscow again became Russia's capital; since then its growth, checked briefly by the Civil War of 1918-20 and the failed German attack of late 1941, has continued irresistibly, oustripping the most ambitious of urban plans and spilling out into areas once designated as green belt. The population now stands at around 9 million.

As part of the 'Stalin Plan for the Reconstruction of Moscow', an underground railway was built and huge avenues were laid out, wide enough to take eight or ten lanes of traffic. The roads in the city centre and along the embankments of the Moskva river are heavily congested, and air pollution is a serious problem. This may surprise foreign visitors who see streets such as Vernadskogo Avenue lined with apple, hazel and pear trees, inner-city areas surrounded by clumps of raspberry canes, or the parks full of wild mushrooms. People make full use of these sources of food – indeed they often plant them. Much of the land around urban apartment blocks is used as kitchen gardens or orchards, which are as carefully tended as any allotments in Britain or the rest of Europe.

This reflects the food shortages that have dogged the Soviet Union throughout its 70-year history, and also the fact that many city dwellers have only recently left the land. Up to 70 per cent of Muscovites have moved to the city in the last one or two generations. This may account for their abruptness and reserve, as they have not had time to develop the social ease that comes from a long tradition of urban living.

The architecture grows uglier as you move out from the centre of Moscow. Suburban sprawl and tower blocks are as much a feature of Communist as of capitalist town planning. Yet this kind of building, already unfashionable in the West in the early 1980s, was vigorously defended until quite recently in the Soviet Union. 'We build upwards to save space. We refuse to build on all the available sites in order to leave land free for parks. The desire for separate houses or small blocks of flats makes no sense in social terms.' Plausible as this argument may sound, it is the view of

Draughts (above) and chess (left) are two of the Russians' favourite games, which they play outdoors whenever they can. Moscow's Gorky Park is a popular gathering point for players.

the administrator rather than the user, and it will be interesting to see whether this philosophy survives the death of Communism.

The big cities have highly-developed public transport systems, with overlapping networks of underground and overground railways, buses, trams, trolleybuses, fixed-route taxis and ordinary cabs. In Moscow, whose Motorway Ring is 70 miles long, such a system is essential. Muscovites spend around two hours a day travelling between home and work. Their journeys are made more uncomfortable by the large numbers of country people who come into town each day either to shop or to sell produce. This practice caused so much discontent that in the summer of 1990, Gavriil Popov, Mayor of Moscow, banned the sale to visitors of goods in short supply, restricting them to people who could prove they were residents of the capital. The Muscovites welcomed these measures.

The 'just in case' bag

City dwellers also spend a great deal of time just looking for food. Both in the heyday of Communism and in the *perestroika* years of Mikhail Gorbachev, food distribution was a problem. (Under Gorbachev, it was said, the only thing that changed about the food shortages was that people could talk about them freely.) The shops ran out of other products too – from clothing to books. No one could ever be sure when the trickle of supply would start or stop, so people carried with them a plastic 'just in case' bag, just in case they should come across something they had been after for days or weeks.

The 'just in case' habit made the situation worse. When large quantities of a certain product reached a

Marriage is still popular despite a high divorce rate, and weddings are elaborate affairs, with hired limousines and gargantuan feasts. In Moscow couples traditionally lay a wreath at the Tomb of the Unknown Soldier.

The biggest McDonald's in the world, with 800 seats, opened in Moscow in 1990. Crowds of young people continue to pour in, despite prices they can barely afford.

'Matrioshka' dolls are more than mere tourist souvenirs; they are also educational toys, used to teach young children to count. The largest contain up to 20 dolls.

This Labour Day (May 1) march shows that Moscow workers are no longer afraid to express their views. Banners read 'Let us work', 'Enough experiments' and 'Real salaries for real work'.

shop in one district, the news soon spread and people from other districts came flocking in. Everyone would buy as much as they could afford of the product, to stock up the freezer, to give or sell to friends, or to exchange with a neighbour for other goods that he, in turn, had bought 'just in case'. Wardrobes, kitchen cupboards and store rooms in millions of urban flats were cluttered with these stockpiles. The effect of such parallel distribution alongside the hopeless official network of the state simply increased shortages.

The grapevine

The Russians are famously hospitable. They lose no opportunity for conviviality, particularly when there is a sniff of vodka in the air. Where else would you start off the evening with one friend, who takes you to visit another friend, and end up with people you have never met before, having lost your original friend somewhere along the line?

It is at such spontaneous social gatherings – which are not restricted to any particular class – that rumours start to circulate, and news spreads before it has appeared in the press or on television. They are also the forum for the exchange of *anyekdoty*, irreverent stories and jokes about the leadership – a safety-valve for people's frustrations, especially in the time of Communist repression and official censorship.

One such joke became a classic at the height of Brezhnev's power in the 1970s. One day, Comrade Brezhnev, proud of all his achievements, invited his mother to visit him in Moscow. He took her in his black Zil limousine round all the great sights. His old mother just frowned. He whisked her out to his spacious country *dacha*. Still she frowned and said nothing. Back to the Kremlin, where he showed her his huge office and the state apartments, introduced her to several

GUM, Moscow's largest and grandest department store, has 150 shops on three levels and tends to be crowded with shoppers from outside the city.

ministers and treated her to lunch served by fawning waiters. His mother looked grim. Desperate to please her, he called for a helicopter to fly them over the city. Brezhnev's mother looked grimmer than ever. Finally, the furious Brezhnev said, 'Why are you looking so glum? All this is mine! See what your son Leonid has achieved! Aren't you pleased?'

'I'm afraid, Leonid.'

'Afraid? Of what?'

'All this is magnificent – but what's going to happen if the Communists get back into power?'

There were many such stories, sharp and devastating satires on a corrupt system of government. Often they spread by telephone – an instrument much loved by the Russians, and an absolute necessity for the kind of hectic social life that reflects the exciting political changes of recent years.

Before *glasnost* (openness) and the freeing of the media from strict state control, news would spread unofficially by telephone at fantastic speed. An example of this 'grapevine' in action concerns the poet and protest singer Vladimir Vysotsky. He was hated by Party officials, who nevertheless failed to have his songs banned. His mocking or nostalgic lyrics, his tobacco-and-vodka-scarred voice, his gifts as an actor and the whiff of rebellion and scandal that he always carried with him made Vysotsky a great popular hero. (Since 1986 his success has become official, with the publication of all his poetry and the re-issue of his records.) One night in July 1980 friends had gathered at someone's house, eating *zakuski* – snacks often taken instead of dinner – when the telephone rang. The hostess answered it, and the look on her face made everyone freeze. 'Vysotsky's dead.'

What a terrible shock: he was so young. Someone put on an early Vysotsky cassette, and people began humming softly to it. Someone found a guitar, and a small, sad group of singers formed. Discreetly, a guest

Moscow women queueing outside a dress shop. Despite the drab 1950s air of this example, private dressmakers' shops are making a big comeback in the larger towns.

A flower-seller in Nevski Prospekt, St Petersburg. Russians adore cut flowers and are willing to spend large amounts on them for festivals such as International Women's Day.

picked up the phone to call a friend, then another friend, then another: 'Have you heard? Vysotsky's dead.'

In between calls, the phone rang.

'Have you heard? Vysotsky's dead.'

'Yes, we know ...'

By early morning, the news had spread to every city in the Soviet Union, before the television, radio or newspapers had reported it.

Two days later, tens of thousands of Muscovites were queueing up outside the Taganka Theatre to pay their last respects to Vysotsky. Many waited for hours. Among them, with roses in their hands and tears in their eyes, were several soldiers. Yet the ceremony was never officially announced.

Entertainment, old and new

Even before Gorbachev's arrival on the scene, lovers of rock music in Russia had their own native superstar, Alla Pugacheva, a woman of extraordinary talents who writes her own lyrics and music. Outside her apartment block in Gorky Street, at 11 o'clock on a July evening, a group of young fans waits for her to appear, knowing that she is there from the white Mercedes parked at the entrance. Finally, after midnight, she appears, leading her basset hound (a rare breed in Russia). The fans make a dash for her, and she signs a few autographs before getting into her car.

In her apartment there is a white piano, a bar, a large false fireplace, exotic fruits, champagne, vodka, diamonds, a top-quality sound-system, a maid with a white apron – in short, the full paraphernalia of a star. Some evenings, after vodka, champagne and *zakuski*, she sits down at her white piano and improvises songs in her gravelly voice. She dazzles and dismays, flitting from virtuoso brilliance to shallow and flashy vulgarity. These sessions can sometimes last all night.

Her devoted fans flock to the concerts given by this forty-year-old sex-bomb of Soviet rock, who studied at the best music schools before finding her own original style: a noisy, violent sound, both on stage and in the recording studio. With her band playing at ear-shattering levels behind her she dances, shouts, struts and flings herself about, suggestively stroking the microphone and whipping her audience into a frenzy.

Until recently, Pugacheva was unique. In a land where life was drab and difficult, popular heroes were lonely figures. Since 1986 the artistic scene and quality of entertainment in the theatre, cinema and on television have been transformed. New talent has mushroomed. Television, freed by liberal legislation, now offers an exciting choice of variety shows, drama, pop music and documentaries. There has been an explosion of rock and new wave music to the especial delight of those who spend Saturday nights either in night clubs or in front of the television.

These changes have not been welcomed by everyone. Those of a conservative disposition fear that young people's minds may be overwhelmed by the gimmickry and corrupt moral values of the West. The traditional performing arts – opera, ballet, theatre, classical and folk music – are a source of pride to such people.

The Bolshoi in Moscow and the Kirov (now Mariinsky) in St Petersburg (to mention only the two best known – there are also ballet companies in each of the former Soviet republics) are both based in magnificent theatres, with reputations founded on rigorous technical training dating back to the 18th century. Throughout the 19th century, ballet was regarded as a serious art in Russia and encouraged by the imperial court, while it went into decline in the West. It was here that the full-scale narrative ballet was developed under dancing masters such as Didelot and Petipa, who choreographed *The Sleeping Beauty*, *Swan Lake* and *The Nutcracker*. In the 20th century the Russians have produced such famous dancers as Anna Pavlova, Vaslav Nijinsky, Michel Fokine, Galina Ulanova, Rudolf Nureyev and Mikhail Baryshnikov; and undoubtedly the most influential figure in 20th-century ballet has been the impresario Serge Diaghilev, whose *Ballets Russes*, which operated from Paris in the years 1909-29, provided a meeting point for some of the greatest composers and artists of the time.

Traditionally-minded Russians, who queue to see the Bolshoi, love folk song and dance and venerate Prokofiev, Mussorgsky, Tchaikovsky and Shostakovich, are saddened by Russian youth rejecting all this for the sake of American-style pop music.

Cities that look down on the capital

St Petersburg was founded in 1703 as a military base against the Swedes by Peter the Great, who moved his capital here nine years later, bringing with him a sometimes reluctant court, with nobles, merchants and diplomatic staff. Throughout the 18th century, the city continued to grow, with the construction of magnificent

The restaurant at Moscow's Kazan Station – a good place for a leisurely meal in palatial surroundings, but not if you're in a hurry to catch a train.

One of Moscow's many markets, selling fresh produce from collective farms (kolkhozy) or private allot-ments. Prices here tend to be higher, but so is the quality.

palaces, embankments and avenues, as befitted an imperial capital. In the 19th century came industrialisation and further expansion: the population grew from 470,000 in 1840 to 2,200,000 in 1914. In response to anti-German feeling during the First World War, the name was Russified to 'Petrograd'. It was here that the two revolutions of 1917 began: the overthrow of the Romanov Tsar Nicholas II in February, and the Bolshevik revolution in October. In 1924, when Lenin died, the city was renamed Leningrad in his honour. From September 1941 to January 1944, for a total of 872 days (but it was called the 900 Day Siege) Leningrad was besieged by the German army. Despite terrible suffering – from shelling, starvation, disease and cold – the city never fell. After the war, Leningrad was energetically reconstructed, with residential suburbs to the north and south. The historic centre was restored, with virtually no high-rise building allowed: an enlightened policy which contrasts with much postwar town-planning in Britain. In 1991, the original name of St Petersburg was restored by popular demand.

This extraordinary city, built on more than a hundred islands of the River Neva delta, is one of the architectural wonders of the world. After a century of social, cultural and political upheaval, the 4.5 million inhabitants are deeply conscious of their city's greatness, and think of themselves as superior to the Muscovites, whom they regard as 'peasants'.

The feeling is shared in other cities along the Baltic: in Tallinn, capital of Estonia, a sense of local pride has been sharpened by resentment at fifty years of foreign rule. In the red-roofed city centre, where many of the houses are between three and four hundred years old, and beautifully maintained and restored, there is a powerful sense of belonging to an older and better culture than the Soviet model brought in with Stalin's armies at the end of the Second World War. 'In Moscow,' they say, 'they haven't got our quiet streets, or our old bookshops, their cafés aren't anything like ours ...' Here indeed the café atmosphere is more

Russian women do many jobs that most Western countries still think too heavy for them: working on building sites, breaking ice and shovelling snow in the streets, and operating heavy machinery. They also have more managerial jobs. Few Russian men, however, are prepared to help in the home.

mellow and subdued than in Moscow. Café life is as popular during the long 'white nights' of summer as it is in winter when the picturesque narrow streets have turned into hazardous skating rinks.

As in Tallinn, so in Riga and Vilnius, the capitals of Latvia and Lithuania. Added to their own national traditions is a strong sense of belonging to the West, both culturally and geographically. This has been reinforced by the availability of Western television channels. The determination of these three republics to break away from Moscow, as expressed in their 1990 declarations of independence, was one of the crucial events in the disintegration of the Soviet Union.

In some ways, the wave of nationalist feeling that has swept across the old USSR has come not a moment too soon. Despite its inefficiency, repression and corruption, and the loathing in which it was held by many, the Communist system has deeply affected the thinking of non-Russians as well as Russians. Its effect on the environment too has been profound. Cities were beginning to resemble one another all over the Soviet Union. Even Kiev, the Ukrainian capital, despite its

glorious Orthodox churches with their green and gold domes, is strongly reminiscent of Moscow. The huge residential tower blocks lining the banks of the River Dnepr are unmistakably in the grim Soviet style.

Our lady of the flowers

A few years ago, the sense of uniformity seemed to trigger a reaction among Soviet city-dwellers. The women in particular began to cultivate more up-to-date, glitzy styles of dress. In winter, when people have to wrap up in thick coats and headscarves, the change is barely noticeable, but in summer the difference has started to show. The girls blossom. Skirts are shorter, colours bolder and T-shirts with slogans in Russian, English or French are all the rage. If you visit friends, they no longer ask you to bring tights but the latest creams and scrubs and lotions from the cosmetic empires of the West. It does no good explaining that the claims made for these products in the advertisements of women's magazines may be a trifle exaggerated: you

Gigantic hoardings like these used to adorn every city, proclaiming the workers' desire for international peace and brotherhood. They have now practically disappeared.

are simply wasting your breath. You will probably be asked for dress-making magazines too, the most popular being the German *Burda-Moden* (now published quarterly in Russia).

Considering that life is such a struggle, the city women have been remarkably resourceful in seizing on the latest Western fashions. Women were long ago liberated in the work-place, but socially they have remained very much the inferiors. Fathers and husbands have the upper hand. Childcare, shopping, cooking and cleaning are still the domain of women, except on International Women's Day (March 8), when men take over the kitchen for the day. 'Modern' couples, where household work is shared, are rare even among the young. Many women are plagued by their husbands' alcoholism, which is responsible for the increasing contempt felt by urban women towards men. Feminists argue that the country would come to a standstill without them. Many economists agree.

If the urban family appears threatened by marital tensions (made worse by alcoholism and poverty), there is no decrease in the number of courting couples in the streets and parks. Fifteen years ago, something as innocent as kissing in public was considered bad taste,

though nowadays only an old country *babushka* on her way to church would bat an eyelid.

Courtship requires flowers, nowhere more so than in Russia. In the last decade the cities have witnessed the rapid growth of a new trade: the unlicensed flower-seller. People from the suburbs and countryside have taken to growing and selling them on a semi-professional basis. It must be a lucrative trade too: few Russians, men or women, can resist a bunch of flowers, and you never see a militiaman confronting a flower-seller or demanding to see his or her licence.

All this encouraged 'wholesalers' of Georgian origin to move in and set up networks of flower-sellers in the cities of Moscow, Leningrad, Tallinn, Minsk and Odessa. This did not go down well with the independent flower-sellers and the experiment was dropped. Then, in 1980, the Georgian florists had a once-in-a-lifetime idea. Two days before International Women's Day (when flower prices always rise dramatically), they filled every street corner and Metro station entrance with beautiful wild flowers – almost too beautiful given the cold weather and the distance they had travelled. Thousands of people bought them, only to find that they disintegrated when they got them home and into vases.

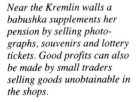

Near the Kremlin walls a babushka supplements her pension by selling photographs, souvenirs and lottery tickets. Good profits can also be made by small traders selling goods unobtainable in the shops.

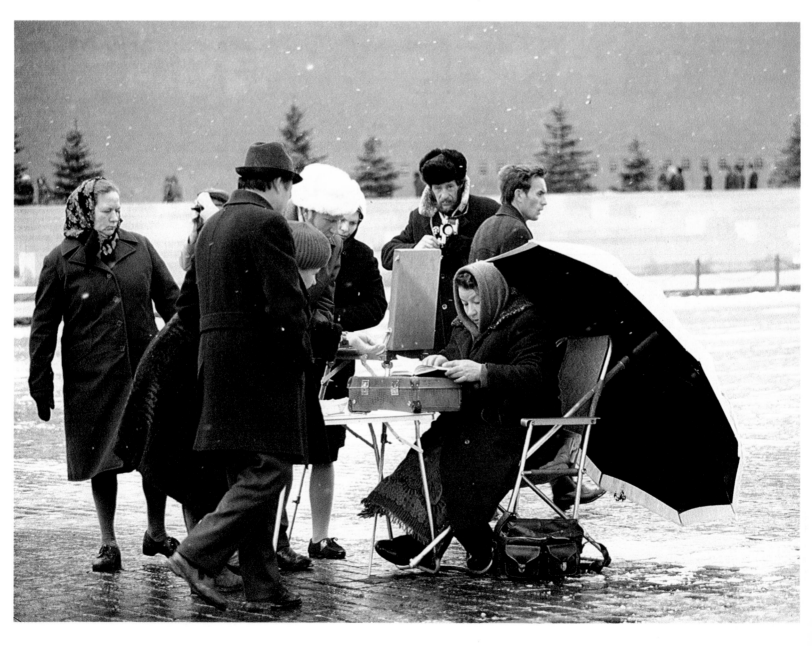

The flowers had been sprayed with hair lacquer. The Georgians were finally discredited – and, not surprisingly, there was a shortage of hairspray in Moscow for months afterwards.

A Russian David Bellamy

When they are not out working or in search of provisions, people in the big cities (like most inhabitants of the developed world) spend a good deal of their time sitting in front of their televisions. The first transmissions were made in 1931, but nationwide broadcasting – making early use of satellite systems to penetrate the farthest reaches of the Union – began in the 1960s. With each republic having its own local language channel as well as the Russian channels from Leningrad and Moscow, the Soviet state broadcasting monopoly – Gosteleradio – could boast programmes in seventy languages. But it was also one of the dullest television services in the world, watched principally for its dramas (including a celebrated Sherlock Holmes series shot in Leningrad), and for its sports and foreign news broadcasts.

After 1986, the situation at Gosteleradio changed radically, with hard-hitting news and current-affairs programmes about waste, crime and corruption, documentaries setting the record straight about Stalin, Khrushchev and Brezhnev; and phone-ins where bureaucrats were confronted with angry callers demanding to know why the industries and services they ran were so inefficient. Television, press and radio were key instruments in Gorbachev's policy of *glasnost*.

One survivor from the old days, and an exception to the general run of drabness, is *In the World of Animals*, hosted for the past fifteen years by Nikolai Drozdov, Professor of Bio-Geography at Moscow University. Drozdov is one of the great naturalist-eccentrics, taking well-publicised swims in ice-covered ponds, picking up scorpions, fondling snakes, and even attempting to ride a rhinoceros. Behind the showman is a deeply-committed conservationist who tries to make his 100 million viewers aware of the beauty of the natural world and of its threatened status. In the immensity of the Soviet Union, with its seven climatic zones ranging from arctic tundra to desert, the variety of habitats and species is enormous. *In the World of Animals* covers golden eagles in Byelorussia, black-headed gulls on the islands of the Black Sea, the great bustard, the monitor lizard, and the Indian racer snake of Turkmenia. Many of these figure in the Soviet 'red data book' of endangered species. Drozdov's speciality is the wildlife of the deserts of Central Asia, the lizards, snakes, spiders and various aggressive insects. His humorous and affectionate commentaries on the lives of these animals combine entertainment with public education.

Fun in the snow

On a winter's day, Moscow's parks are full of cross-country skiers and people towing their children around on toboggans. You will also see men breaking the ice on ponds and swimming in the freezing black water. Others will strip to the waist and rub their bare chests with snow in displays of virility.

The snow slows down the pace of life everywhere. There is no point in fighting it, and Muscovites are masters at adapting to it. The first permanent snow comes in November, with further falls up to the end of March, although occasionally they will persist until May. During this period of the year, the climate determines both people's behaviour and their appearance. Whether it is cold (-3° to -5°C) or very cold (-20° to -25°C), nobody goes out without a fur hat with

City dwellers make the most of the snow in winter, tobogganing, skating and skiing in the parks.

A winter's day on the River Neva in St Petersburg (formerly Leningrad). The city stands on more than 100 islands in the Neva delta. Here, people have drilled holes in the ice and hung fishing lines into the unfrozen waters beneath – their catches are often surprisingly large.

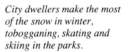

ear-muffs – a *chapka* – or some other protective headgear. Ears have a nasty habit of freezing up if left uncovered for long at low temperatures. The victim is often unaware that his ears are frozen until a friend or passer-by points out that they have changed colour. No pain is felt however, until thawing-out is attempted – and then it hurts.

Russia's winters may be harsh but they are also very beautiful, especially in those parts of the cities that have retained their traditional character. Some of St Petersburg's grandest streets verge on the sublime when the snow starts to settle. At times during these white winters you have the curious sensation that Anton Chekhov might just step out of a doorway, or suddenly appear on a station platform beside you. Yet it could equally be the young Lenin, or Pushkin, or Catherine the Great ...

The abacus is still widely used by tradespeople and bank clerks, who operate it with great agility. Even when a calculator is available, the result will often be checked manually – on an abacus.

The Russian Orthodox Church

Winter also means Christmas for a growing number of Russian Orthodox Christians, and indeed for those who now feel free to celebrate their old traditions again. Since the liberalisation of Soviet society under Gorbachev, the Orthodox Church has seen a great revival in its fortunes. In 1988, to mark the thousandth anniversary of the coming of Christianity to Russia, Moscow's Danilov Monastery (founded in 1272, rebuilt by Ivan the Terrible, and used as a factory under Communism) was returned to the Church as a new headquarters. Other important properties were given back, as was the right to impart religious instruction to

one's children. Monks came back to Moscow for the first time in seventy years.

Christianity first came to Russia by way of the Slavs of Moravia (a territory that now forms the central part of Czechoslovakia). Two brothers from Thessalonica, Cyril and Methodius, were sent as missionaries from Constantinople in 863 at the request of the Moravian ruler, Prince Rostislav. Cyril and Methodius translated the Bible into the Slavonic language, inventing an alphabet in the process – Cyrillic – which was based on a mixture of Greek and Hebrew characters and is still used in modified form today, in Russian, Ukrainian, Bulgarian and Serbian script. A century and a quarter after the mission of Cyril and Methodius, the Christian gospel reached Kiev, where in 988 Prince Vladimir had all his subjects baptised in the River Dnepr.

At first the Russian Church was supervised by Greeks, but after the fall of Constantinople to the Ottoman Turks in 1453 control passed to the Russians. Moscow was proclaimed 'the third Rome', and in 1589 its Metropolitan (or top Bishop) was promoted to the

rank of Patriarch, fifth in seniority after Constantinople, Alexandria, Antioch and Jerusalem. A close association with the autocratic rule of the Tsars made the Church a conservative, and at times repressive, force in Russian history, with its priests preaching unquestioning submission to the state. The Church was also nationalistic, promoting the concept of 'Holy Russia' and teaching its congregations that Russians were particularly favoured by God and that their Tsar was his greatest lieutenant on earth.

The monks, or 'black' clergy, were key figures in the religious life of tsarist Russia; and it was from their ranks that bishops were chosen. The parish priests, or 'white' clergy, were married men who lived and worked with the people of the villages where they were posted for life. There were also *starets* or holy men, some of whom possessed great spiritual power and were said to work miracles; many varieties of strange sects, including 'jumpers' who jumped while praying; *khlysty* or flagellators; and the *doukhobors* who refused to acknowledge earthly authority.

Russian women get together in a café. Under the Communists, women did at least manage to carve out an important role for themselves, especially in Russia's cultural life.

A vendor in Lomonosov Square, St Petersburg, selling kvas – *a popular Russian form of beer made from fermented buckwheat, rye, wheat and sugar.*

The notorious Rasputin was both a *starets* and a *khlysty*, who refined the 'flagellation' philosophy by claiming that one was closest to God in a state of exhaustion following prolonged sexual intercourse. In the superstitious atmosphere of the court of the last Tsar, Nicholas II, this bizarre figure came to have an enormous influence, gaining credibility through his healing powers over Nicholas's haemophiliac son. Rasputin's debauched behaviour in private, and his disastrous political influence, brought the Church and the imperial family into the lowest possible repute. In December 1916 a group of conspirators led by Prince Yusupov tried to salvage the situation by killing Rasputin. This proved a great deal harder than they had imagined: they tried feeding him poisoned cakes and wine, but these failed to have any effect, so Yusupov shot him; Rasputin still had the strength to run out of the building, so they shot him again in a courtyard, then tied him up and pushed him through a hole in the ice in the River Neva. This did the trick, but they were too late to save the Tsar, who was toppled only two months later.

When the Bolsheviks came to power in October 1917 they realised that the Church could be a dangerous enemy. They issued a decree in February 1918 disestablishing the Church and making all faiths equal before the law. Church land and buildings were nationalised, and religious education was banned. Priests were taxed punitively, and their right to vote taken away. Even meetings of the clergy were allowed only with official permission.

The sable, a member of the weasel family much prized for its fur, comes from the forests of northern Asia. It is now a protected species.

The Trinity Monastery of St Sergius in Zagorsk (now renamed Sergier Posad), about 40 miles from Moscow.

Zagorsk was the most important centre of the Russian Orthodox Church for most of the Soviet period.

The Church had no choice but to accept the Bolshevik régime. Individuals were still free to hold religious beliefs but, with most churches closed and many priests in labour camps or prison, it was hard to worship except in private. The government published books and pamphlets arguing that religion was based on superstition and had been made obsolete by science. The authorities even organised flights in passenger aircraft for the peasants, to prove that there was no heaven above the clouds – until one of the planes crashed and the scheme was called off.

In the 1940s the Church began to regain some of its lost ground by declaring support for Stalin in the fight against the German invaders. In return, Stalin became more lenient towards religious believers, although his successor, Khrushchev, renewed the harsh and violent tactics of the 1920s and 1930s: some 60 per cent of the nation's churches were closed and many demolished. This provoked an angry reaction not only from Christians but from Russian art historians and architects, and the persecutions had the paradoxical effect of strengthening religious belief. A more tolerant attitude was adopted under Brezhnev, though without any change in the legal position. Thus the changes that occurred in 1988, in particular the renewed right of the Church to own property and to give religious instruction, were truly revolutionary events in the Church's history. With twenty thousand churches now functioning and with a religious revival among the young, the Orthodox Church's future now seems assured.

A Russian Orthodox priest – one of the 'black clergy' of monks from whom the senior clerics are selected. The 'white clergy' remain parish priests for life.

The 17th-century buildings of the Novodevichy Convent on the bank of the Moskva river, one of the finest ecclesiastical complexes in Russia. In its cemetery are buried Khrushchev, Gogol, Eisenstein, Stanislavsky, Chekhov, Prokofiev and many other great figures of Russian history.

After dark

Along with a revived interest in religion, Russia and the other western republics have witnessed a sudden boom in spiritualism, including ouija boards and contacts with the dead. People spend whole evenings in earnest conversation with ghosts or the spirits of dead relatives – more in pursuit of scary thrills than spiritual insight. This is more than just a fashion: it is an epidemic spread by word of mouth, without the help of a single magazine or journal. Women are at the forefront of it, offering private courses in spiritualism in the hope of gaining followers and money.

Yoga and vegetarianism have become fashionable, too – the latter prompting the unkind rumour that the craze was started by the government in order to help to cope with the shortage of meat.

Alternative healing is becoming popular. In late 1990, certain 'healers' appeared on television, claiming that they could cure people at a distance. These programmes created such a controversy that they had to be stopped, but the 'healers' in question continue to practise, using stadiums and public theatres.

Tempted by the West, yet suspicious of it, the people of the western republics of the old Soviet Union are ready to try anything that might make life more colourful. Not that they are unhappy – it is more complicated than that: they are looking for something that will enrich their lives, but they are not quite sure what this thing will be. Meanwhile, they struggle for the most part with the same problems and worries that beset their richer counterparts in the West. The quality of education in schools is declining, for example; young people are becoming idle; crime is on the increase; and the streets are unsafe at night.

Meanwhile, the usual Western answer to daily problems – going out and having a good time – has been hard to achieve. Under the Soviet system there was little night life. Public places closed at 10.30pm – not just for reasons of public order, but more because of the puritan streak in socialist thinking. The State could only organise collective pleasures, not individual ones.

Supposing one wanted an evening out in Moscow – what would be available? First of all there is the Bolshoi ballet and opera: though regularly sold out, tickets for tourists in the splendid 2000-seat theatre can usually be found. If you can't get in to the Bolshoi, however, there is also the Moisseiev ballet, which is almost as popular. Rock music and jazz are thriving, meanwhile, with excellent bands performing in Palaces of Culture and clubs all over Moscow. Rock concerts are held in the Green Theatre in Gorky Park or the Olympic Stadium. The best jazz venue in Moscow is the Bluebird Café in Ulitsa Chekhova. For orchestral and chamber music, Muscovites go to the Tchaikovsky Conservatoire, the Tchaikovsky Concert Hall, or the Rossiya Theatre which hosts gala concerts.

The restaurant scene is changing rapidly, with the introduction of co-operative and ethnic establishments, but even though prices have climbed steeply there is a much greater variety of food and ambience now than there was in the bad old days, when the most that a visitor could expect was endless borshch and chicken Kiev in restaurants that felt like aircraft hangars.

The soaring population of Moscow is largely made up of migrants from the country-side. It is estimated that up to 70 per cent have arrived within the past one or two generations.

Along the Trans-Siberian Railway

When the Trans-Siberian grinds to a halt at Irkutsk (about two-thirds of the way along the 5,787-mile journey from Moscow to Vladivostok) you step out on to the platform, and at once a mass of half-remembered pictures from books and films fills your mind. The scene before you is exactly like something out of a traveller's tale. It is as exotic as anything you can imagine, only much more exciting, for it is real.

Irkutsk station is like a noisy caravanserai. Every ten minutes, day and night, a train passes through, carrying passengers or goods. In the station hall, above the waiting travellers with their parcels and badly-shut suitcases, huge clocks remind everyone of the time in the cities they are heading for, or the cities they left a few hours or maybe days ago.

As for the time in Irkutsk itself – like other great railway stations of the past century, it seems to stand above time, gigantic and eternal. Go to one of the second-hand bookstalls in a tiny yellow-and-green *izba* (wooden house) opposite and buy a few old postcards: there stands the station, exactly as it is now, in a picture dated perhaps 1908.

The bustle of Irkutsk underlines an important point about the Trans-Siberian: it is not a railway to the edge of the world, a romantic relic kept going for the sake of foreign tourists who want to get to Japan by the scenic route; it is a heavily used goods and passenger line connecting the two ends of Russia.

Several miles before you reach Irkutsk, escorting you in as it were, a river runs alongside the track. This is the Angara, and it flows out of Lake Baikal, the deepest lake in the world.

Baikal contains one-fifth of the world's surface fresh water and is fed by 336 rivers and streams. It is 395 miles long, up to a mile deep in places, and an average of 30 miles wide. It is surrounded by mountains, rising up to 6500 feet high, in a geological formation that is more than 500 million years old. It contains some 1200 species of animals and 600 species of plants, around three-quarters of which are not found anywhere else in the world.

The lake's waters are safe to drink and extraordinarily clear. In the 1970s, in response to the threat to their purity posed by factories around the shores, there arose the first successful defiance of the Soviet authorities by a coalition of concerned citizens: including lawyers, scientists, writers, artists and academics. As a result of their campaign, purification equipment was put into the factories and all polluting discharges into the lake ceased.

Baikal determines the climate around it, making the weather less extreme than it would otherwise be in that part of the world. The average air temperature in mid-winter is -19°C, and in mid-summer 11°C. Even so, Siberia is in the permafrost zone, where the earth below two yards deep is permanently frozen. Large buildings have to be supported on thermally insulated piles so that they do not melt their way down through the supporting

The izba *is a traditional wooden house with painted shutters and often beautifully carved window-frames. They are now protected buildings.*

A village of izbas *between Irkutsk and Lake Baikal. People here live by farming, timber felling, livestock rearing and fishing in the River Angara.*

earth. Siberians become alarmed when they see foreigners stretching out on the grass to bask in the summer sun: they know that the depths of the earth harbour a harmful and insidious cold, and that nature is not quite as friendly as it looks.

The Angara, a tributary of the Yenisey, is the only river that flows out of Lake Baikal. It is a calm, majestic waterway, along which the fishermen ply their trade all year round in defiance of the elements: in July and August they cast lines from their boats as they bat away the mosquitoes; and in winter, when the temperature is -25°C, they cut holes in the ice in order to catch fish which then freeze to death the moment they make contact with the air.

Irkutsk started life as a winter camp, set up in the mid-17th century during the Russian colonisation of Siberia. It quickly grew into a thriving town thanks to its position on the main trade route between Russia and China. With the coming of the Trans-Siberian Railway at the end of the 19th century, Irkutsk expanded again to become an industrial, administrative and cultural centre of more than half a million inhabitants.

Despite modernisation and the usual faceless suburbs, the heart of the city has kept many of its narrow tree-lined streets, with their brightly painted wooden houses

Women fill the ranks of the army, police and customs officials but do not yet share equally in senior positions of command. The same is generally true in politics, where female leaders are rare.

surrounded by kitchen gardens which are alive with rabbits and chickens. The streets and embankments along the Angara are bustling and cheerful. The people come from a surprising variety of backgrounds and regions: Asia, Europe and the Mediterranean. Here in Irkutsk, as in other Siberian cities to the north and east, a new Russian nation is coming into being, just as during the last century a new American nation was formed on the western frontiers of the United States. The inhabitants of Siberia are strongly aware of this, and they speak with considerable pride of being pioneers and making their homeland out of vast open spaces of virgin territory.

Young and old in Siberia

Just downstream from Irkutsk is a large hydro-electric dam. Passenger boats run trips here in the summer months, stopping at a surprising place for Siberia – an open-air night-club overlooking the water. This is where young people come to dance on summer evenings. Alcohol is strictly forbidden, but this appears to make little difference to the wild atmosphere generated by the loud rock bands. The dancers are mainly couples, though single boys, or the occasional girl in tight jeans and high heels, will often get up and dance alone, absorbed in the music.

In Moscow such behaviour is more or less accepted by the older generation, but out here in the provinces it verges on the scandalous. Girls are expected to know their place and behave with dignity. Many remove their make-up before returning home.... And yet, just when one is thinking how reminiscent all this is of small-town America in the fifties, and how much more 'advanced' we are in the West, one is reminded that here in Siberia

The main square in
Khabarovsk, eastern Siberia –
although it could, with its
anonymous architecture, be
practically anywhere in Russia.

Municipal gardeners in
Irkutsk plant flowers along
the streets. The summer is so
short here that when it comes
the locals are determined to
make the most of it.

there are women company directors, women politicians, engineers, doctors and university professors.

Young and old are not always at peace in Siberia. Even among the Buryats – Mongolian herdsmen with a highly developed social order – many of the young are disassociating themselves from the past. They feel ashamed of their culture, and think only of imitating the Muscovites. It is hard to persuade them that they belong to a dignified people with valuable traditions.

The Buryats can still be seen galloping across the taiga as they herd their flocks, or riding along the banks of the Angara, always leaning well forward in their saddles. More rarely will you see them in their festival costumes. These festivals, with sacred fires and songs, are another source of embarrassment to the Moscow-fixated youth. They speak of them as 'savage rituals' and seem bewildered when anyone from outside shows any interest in them.

Other young Siberians, including some Buryats, think differently. With the recent upheavals in Soviet society

they have begun to rediscover their roots and take pride in themselves as members of separate nations. They cultivate their ethnic identity as a form of individualism, a defiance of central authority.

Many of these young people read the works of a Siberian author called Valentin Rasputin, whose reputation has spread far beyond his native land. He wants to keep alive the best of the past, and has campaigned for the preservation of traditional architecture as well as adding his voice to the protests about the pollution of Lake Baikal. His books are deeply rooted in Siberian life. In *Farewell to Matyora*, for example, he tells of an old village which has to be evacuated for the construction of a huge dam. It is a harsh and agonising book which expresses the doubts of Siberians about the meaning of 'progress' – an ambiguous term to all classes and ages, peasants, workers and intellectuals alike. It also makes one realise that Siberia is not quite so 'exotic': their problems are surprisingly similar to ours.

The joyous Georgians

Just as the first snow is starting to settle on the shores of Lake Baikal, grapes are being harvested in Georgia. It is a time of celebration. The picking is done largely by hand, and the atmosphere is cheerful as the gangs of helpers set off each day to gather the fruit. The labour of local workmen and women is supplemented by students who come down to Georgia for the season to earn a few extra roubles.

At the end of the harvest comes the feasting. The people wear traditional costumes and bring out their

In northern Siberia, reindeer-farming is practised by Lapps in the Murmansk region and by Asians. Reindeer are used both as draught-animals and for meat, and their hides are made into tents, clothing and boots.

The troika, a sleigh pulled by three horses, is no longer a common sight, even though it remains the most reliable form of transport in snowy weather.

musical instruments. The display of food is magnificent, including every conceivable kind of *zakuski*, *shashlik* (meat grilled on skewers), pork charcuterie, whole roast sheep and Georgian-style pickled chicken. The wines are varied and good: with over five hundred varieties of grape, Georgia is the largest producer of wine in the former Soviet Union. The white wines are generally regarded as the best (Tsinandali and Gurdzhani are particularly good), with a pleasing balance of sharpness and fruit. Mukudzani, Saperavi and Napareuli are also very palatable dry red wines, and, for curiosity value, there are the sweeter Hvanchkara and Kinzma'aruli reds, which were Stalin's favourite wines.

At these feasts you see just how much the Georgians love to eat and drink. Their recipes often use mouth-watering combinations of the most surprising ingredients: chicken or lamb with walnuts, prunes, basil, coriander, parsley and pomegranate juice (*kharcho*); or pheasant cooked in Malmsey wine and green tea with oranges, grapes and walnuts. They have maintained this tradition even when there were shortages elsewhere. A Georgian would feel disgraced if he could not track down foodstuffs in short supply.

Georgians pride themselves on their ability to get by. The most resourceful Muscovite is an amateur compared to the average citizen of Tbilisi. If a tourist needs a battery for his camera, even an unusual one, a Georgian will find one within hours. In Moscow or St Petersburg it might take two days.

Once the meal is over, and provided there is at least one guest among the party, it is time for the toasts. Whether you are in a big hotel, or someone's flat, or at one end of a barn, the ritual is endless: a toast to the women, a toast to friendship, a toast to the harvest, to the dancers, to the weather today and the weather tomorrow, to the new wine, or to the horseman about to set off for the mountains. At the end of the table sits the toastmaster, who passes requests on to the head of the family. When there is more than one table you may find several sub-toastmasters being appointed to communicate with the master.

These toasting sessions have been known to take a bizarre turn. Someone may raise a final glass to a famous Georgian who passed away in 1953: Joseph Vissarionovich Dzugashvili, better known as Stalin. The name never fails to send a shock-wave through any Russians who may be present. They generally take this as a signal to leave discreetly....

Georgians have mixed feelings about their most famous son, and the museum to Stalin at his birthplace in Gori has now been closed. They have no such ambivalence about their other achievements. Georgian industry produces hydroelectric power, sheet metal, steel, seamless piping, railway locomotives and heavy vehicles. Despite its mountainous terrain, Georgia's fertile soil and sunny climate permit them to export tea, tobacco, orchard fruits, sugar beet, grain, tinned food and dairy products. The cultural heritage is rich too. Their written language dates back to the 5th century AD, and their architectural treasures attract many tourists. The Georgians call themselves Kartveli – the name 'Georgia' comes from the Persian *Gorj* – and their region Sakartvelo.

The capital, Tbilisi (Tiflis in Persian) is known by the locals as Kalaki ('the town'). It was founded as the Georgian capital in the 5th century AD and, because of its strategic position, occupied or sacked by Persians, Byzantines, Mongols and Turks. The Russians took over the city in 1801.

The grape harvest in Georgia – the high-point of the agricultural year, a time of feasting and celebration. Georgia manages to produce much of the food it consumes, with enough left over for export. The rising tide of nationalism, however, means that the Georgians are reluctant to export to their old fellows in the former Soviet Union, especially Russia and the Ukraine.

A village street in Georgia. Don't be deceived by the appearance: Georgian farming is highly successful, and the envy of other republics.

*The Russians still like to
camp the old-fashioned way,
with food from the wild
cooked on wood fires.
Millions of them go 'back to
nature' this way every
summer, but they are starting
to cause concern among
ecologists and wardens of
nature reserves and
national parks.*

The old town, by the river Kura, has been preserved,
and the cultural life of Tbilisi is impressive, with a
university and several excellent museums: among them
the Museum of Georgian Art, which has gold jewellery
from ancient Colchis; 12th-century enamels from the
reign of Queen Tamara; and the marvellous naïve
paintings of Niko Pirosmanashvili. Also based in Tbilisi
is the world-renowned Rustaveli Theatre Company.

One cannot speak of the Georgians without
mentioning their intense nationalist feeling. It was this
that led a crowd of 20,000 to gather in Tbilisi in May
1978 to protest against a new constitution which
threatened to reduce the status of their language and
culture. The demonstration took place in the tense

Peasants sit at their roadside stalls in the Aragvi valley, Georgia, selling fruit, vegetables and wine. Almost all of this produce is organically grown.

presence of the military but passed off without incident, and the authorities took note: the proposed constitution was changed. This episode was an early indication of the nationalism which was later to prove such a thorn in the side of Gorbachev.

Georgians say that socialism worked in their country because they had the good sense to put the *kolkhozy* (collective farms) high up in the mountains, and the private garden plots in the valleys below: a slight exaggeration that contains an important truth. The Russians confirm it, with their half-admiring, half-resentful tales of Georgians arriving in Moscow with fat wads of roubles in their pockets.

Rich or poor, the Georgians are exciting people to be with: handsome, well-mannered, hospitable, and full of laughter. Whether in the capital, Tbilisi, or in remote country villages, a warm welcome is always guaranteed.

The markets in Tbilisi, the Georgian capital, are gay, noisy and colourful, and the produce – whether from collective farms or private allotments (usually the latter) – is always excellent.

A Georgian family preparing for a christening. The unfortunate sheep being dragged along by its horn will be slaughtered for the feast.

Christian Armenia

Historically, the Armenian people have occupied land now divided between Turkey and the present republic of Armenia. Turkish Armenia, which has no political designation, covers 57,000 square miles, while the former Soviet republic covers 11,500. To the south lies Iran, to the east Azerbaijan, to the north Georgia, and to the west Turkey. In ancient times (beginning in the 6th century BC) Armenia was a powerful kingdom at the junction of the Roman and Persian empires; it later became the first nation to embrace Christianity (in 301). However, the country lost its independence in the 14th century and has since had a tragic history, subjected to a long series of foreign invasions and atrocities. The years between 1870 and 1920 were worse than most: Russia and Turkey were both responsible for massacres of Armenians. In 1915 more than half a million died at the hands of the Turks. In recent times, Armenia has suffered again, with the start of the murderous dispute with neighbouring Azerbaijan over the enclave of Nagorno Karabakh in early 1988 and the massive earthquake in December of the same year.

Despite its grim present and past, Armenia, the smallest of the old Soviet republics, has in peaceful times much the same friendly atmosphere as Georgia. It produces fruit, vegetables, cereals, tobacco, wine, and fine brandies which, it is claimed, rival French cognac in quality. During the Soviet period, the country was successfully industrialised, and became an important producer of textiles, machinery, chemicals and precision instruments.

Yerevan, the Armenian capital since 1920, is an attractive modern city built of volcanic tufa on steep hillsides climbing from the river Razdan. It has a university and a library of world importance in the Matenadaran, with its unique collection of ancient Armenian manuscripts dating from the 5th century AD.

Fourteen miles away, brooding magnificently over the city, stands Mount Ararat, on the far side of the Turkish border. The Armenians call themselves the descendants of Noah, whose ark is said to have landed

This Armenian schoolgirl still wears a traditional school uniform, although children in cities are claiming the right to wear their own clothes.

Yerevan, the Armenian capital, has long been famed for its humorists. In recent years, though, it has lost much of its sparkle, following the earthquake of 1988 and the conflict with Azerbaijan.

between the mountain's two peaks. The whole of Armenia is mountainous – the average height above sea-level is 5400 feet – with a dry continental climate, which probably contributes to the inhabitants' longevity as much as the country's famous yoghurt (which usually gets the credit).

Armenian banquets are lavish affairs, with marvellous yoghurt soups and stews such as *bozbash*, made with lamb, chick peas, tomatoes and onions, together with combinations of red peppers, quinces, apples, damsons, apricots, aubergines and plums. Wine is plentiful, as is *lavas* – the dry, wafer-like bread which brings on a powerful thirst. The Russians claim that *lavas* was invented as a pretext for drinking. While keeping their fine wines and brandies for themselves, the Armenians export the rougher wines to their 'comrades' in Moscow.

Baku – Dallas of Transcaucasia

By the time you reach Azerbaijan, you really begin to feel that you have left Europe. Hot, dry southerly winds blow in from Iran, bringing drought. The summer sun scorches the villages and fields, and the herds of grazing animals are driven high into the mountains to find pastures and cool air. This is unmistakably Asia. Not poor Asia, however, for Azerbaijan is a country that has grown rich on oil.

Around half of Azerbaijan's 7.1 million people now live in cities, and a quarter of them in the capital, Baku – the Dallas of Transcaucasia. Like other Soviet cities, Baku has had to expand quickly. The town planners have struggled to keep up with the demands of economic and demographic growth, and not always succeeded.

Nevertheless, Baku is a pleasant city, laid out in a natural amphitheatre overlooking the Caspian Sea, on which it is the largest port. There is a picturesque old town, surrounded by defensive walls, dating from the city's heyday under the Sirvan Shahs (9th to 13th centuries). A number of handsome 19th-century buildings reflect the oil boom that began in the 1870s: by the early part of the 20th century, Baku was the largest oilfield in the world, and remained the biggest in the Soviet Union until the 1940s. There are also several well-planned modern areas of the city, and some modern buildings – such as the Hotel Azerbaijan – which marry old and new styles of architecture without wholly disastrous results.

At times Baku can seem a little hectic to the traveller, but it is a good city for strolling: there is a two-mile circuit of the old town walls along a pleasant tree-lined boulevard, and from the 12th century Maiden's Tower (Gyz Galasy) there are splendid views over Baku harbour to the Caspian Sea. There is also the Palace of the Shirvan Shahs, now a museum; the 11th-century Synyk-Kala Mosque and Minaret; the Mausoleum of the astronomer Seida Bakuvi; and the labyrinth of narrow streets that comprises the old town.

Azerbaijan's mineral wealth has been famed for hundreds of years. Marco Polo, travelling through the Middle East in the late 13th century, has left us with this

Kazakh fishermen with a catch that includes two fine sturgeon. Strict quotas are now in force to protect the threatened populations of this valuable fish.

Sturgeon are caught as they swim up the River Volga from the Caspian Sea to spawn. Their roe is made into caviar, one of the CIS's major hard currency exports.

A woman selling curd cheese
in a market in Ashkhabad,
capital of Turkmenistan.
Another task for women in this
desert republic is weaving the
famous Turkmen carpets.
Their magnificent colour-sense
can also be seen in their dress.

A Turkmen herdsman riding
bareback and wearing a headdress made from the fleece of
the karakul sheep. A close-up
of this extraordinary hat can
be seen opposite.

A meal in Azerbaijan starts with bowls of yoghurt or buttermilk with raw vegetables and herbs, followed by fruit sautéed in butter. Then come stews such as *galya* – veal with garlic, lentils, almonds, chestnuts and cherries – or a *pilau* (*plov* in Russian), a rice dish combining meat and fruits with fresh herbs. Another speciality to try is *kutab* – a pastry filled with pumpkin or other vegetables. Despite their Muslim faith, the Azerbaijanis make wine, although it is not as good as the wines of Georgia and Armenia.

Three-quarters of the population are Muslim Turkic Azerbaijanis, with Russians the largest minority group. One minority much in the news has been the Armenians who form 80 per cent of the population of Nagorno Karabakh. This region was incorporated in the Soviet Socialist Republic of Azerbaijan for administrative reasons – an unhappy situation which has led to violent conflict.

Insh'Allah

A long, noisy boat ride across the Caspian Sea – the largest inland sea in the world – takes travellers into Central Asia, which consists of the five republics of Turkmenistan, Uzbekistan, Kyrgyzstan, Tajikistan and Kazakhstan.

The boat lands at Krasnovodsk in Turkmenistan. This is the smallest and poorest of the republics, with a population of 3,714,100. The land is 90 per cent desert, of which the Kara-Kum with its famous heat-retaining black sands is the largest. It ends just outside the capital, Ashkhabad.

Ashkhabad is a surprisingly lush city. There are fountains and lakes in the parks, avenues of plane trees, ditches of burbling water running along the streets, and shady courtyards and gardens that offer much-needed protection from the blistering summer heat. The water that makes all this possible comes from the River Amu Darya (known to the ancient world as the Oxus) 500 miles away across the desert, its flow diverted by the Kara-Kum canal to the city.

The artisans' market, held every Thursday in Ashkhabad. Scenes like this give an immediate sense of the distance – in culture, dress, outlook and way of life – between the Central Asian republics and Moscow, despite 70 years of Soviet rule.

Turkmen horses are highly prized for their speed and endurance as well as their beauty. They are widely used by herdsmen raising cattle, sheep, goats and camels.

description: 'Near the Georgian border there is a spring from which gushes a stream of oil, in such abundance that a hundred ships may load there at once. This oil is not good to eat; but it is good for burning and as a salve for men and camels affected with itch or scab. Men come from a long distance to fetch this oil, and in all the neighbourhood no other oil is burnt but this.'

The Baku oilfields are now almost played out, with new wells being drilled offshore in the Caspian Sea. Elsewhere in the country the petroleum and natural gas industries flourish. Other resources include lead, zinc, iron and copper ores, marble and limestone.

Among attractions outside Baku are the Surakhany Fire-worshippers' Temple, and the rock-paintings of Kobustan with their wealth of subjects – battles, dances, animals, ships, planets and people – and graffiti left by legionaries from ancient Rome.

Ashkhabad is barely more than a hundred years old, founded in 1881 as a fort during the Russian invasion of the region. Before then it was a crossroads for caravan routes in the Kopet-Dag Oasis. In 1948 a tremendous earthquake virtually destroyed the place.

Sitting in a courtyard, sipping tea under the cherry trees, you exchange polite conversation with your Turkmen hosts. As night falls, bringing a welcome breath of cooler air from the mountains, the talk begins to run deeper. 'The earthquake? Of course I remember it. It was just after one o'clock in the morning. I was in bed, and I woke up suddenly, with this terrible feeling that my house, the whole town, just didn't exist any more. There was a silence all around that was thick – like glue. I wanted to get up and shout, to release all the tension inside me, and at that moment the earth exploded ... That's what I remember, more than the ruins and the bodies ...'

Until 1924, when the Turkmen Soviet Socialist

The cotton harvest in Uzbekistan, which looks like becoming one of the richest and most powerful of the former Soviet republics. One of its advantages is an abundance of cheap labour.

Republic was formed, the Turkmens were herdsmen living in tribes, with no political or national organisations. This is how Marco Polo described them: 'The Turcomans, who worship Mahomet and keep his law, are a primitive people, speaking a barbarous language. They roam over the mountains and the plains, wherever they know that there is good pasturage, because they live off their flocks. They have clothing made of skins, and dwellings of felt or of skins. The country breeds good Turcoman horses and good mules of excellent quality.'

The Turkmens are proud of their history and traditions, and never thought of themselves as belonging naturally to the former Soviet Union. They admit freely that the Russians have helped them, with irrigation, industry, transport, education and so on, but now they say they have grown up: it is time for them to develop independently.

They will also tell you not to pay too much attention to their cities, for they are soulless. Look instead at the

countryside, the deserts, and the nomads still driving their herds from pasture to pasture. Listen to their tales of long journeys, undertaken when all the tribesmen were wanderers, long before the settlement and cultivation of the oases in the 18th century. It is here that you will find the traditions and customs that will make their future.

In Soviet days, if you came to Turkmenistan from Moscow, the locals would ask you: 'Apart from the fact that people speak Russian here, what other similarity can you see between this place and the country you have just left?' It was never an easy question to answer. They are keen, though, not to be misunderstood, insisting that they had no quarrel with Moscow – only an overwhelming sense of difference, of paths that must inevitably diverge.

If you take an interest in the local culture you will be shown beautiful brightly-coloured costumes and perhaps treated to some tunes on the short native flute – a haunting sound strongly reminiscent of the Andes. You should also try to see the handmade Turkmen carpets which the herdsmen carry rolled on their camel-saddles as they drive their flocks of Karakul sheep. Marco Polo wrote that these carpets were 'the choicest and most beautiful in the world'.

The Turkmens have a proverb, which says 'A woman

who cannot weave a carpet has no right to eat.' The girls who weave them are a lovely sight in themselves, with their gorgeous coloured robes, their almond-shaped eyes the colour of gilded copper, and their braided hair ornamented with antique silver coins.

Turkmenia exports carpets to more than fifty countries around the world. The designs vary from tribe to tribe, and you can get an idea of the range from the display at the Museum of Fine Arts in Ashkhabad. The carpets take their names from the tribes that weave them, most having a *gul* or tribal motif. Ersari carpets are the exception to this rule; they have no *gul* but use a variety of patterns, including diamond lattices and stylised palm-trees, in striking combinations of colours that typically include yellow, brown and contrasting shades of blue. The Salor rugs, usually designed as large storage bags, are predominantly red, woven of wool or goat hair, with the *gul* (an elaborate octagon, often embellished with silk threads) in the centre. The Tekke carpets, which have a small lozenge-shaped *gul* arranged in rows on a grid of blue lines over a background of rich crimson, are the finest and most highly prized of all.

There is much to recommend a visit to Turkmenistan, including the Bakharden Cave, with its amazing underground lake (at a constant temperature of 36°C it is ideal for swimming), and the medieval city of Merv, where Omar Khayyam ran the observatory in the 11th century. Omar is known in the West as a poet, largely through the sonorous Victorian 'translation' (actually an assembly of dozens of separate four-line poems skilfully threaded together) by Edward Fitzgerald. But his fame during his lifetime rested on his mastery of an astonishing range of subjects: mathematics, history, medicine, law, philosophy and astronomy.

One could do worse than leave the ex-Soviet Socialist Republic of Turkmenistan with this sobering reflection on the fate of earthly empires, from the *Rubaiyat of Omar Khayyam*:

'The Worldly Hope men set their Hearts upon
Turns Ashes – or it prospers; and anon,
Like Snow upon the Desert's dusty Face,
Lighting a little Hour or two – is gone...
Think, in this batter'd Caravanserai
Whose Doorways are alternate Night and Day,
How Sultan after Sultan with his Pomp
Abode his Hour or two, and went his way.'

The timeless face of Uzbekistan: nomadic herdsmen, who continue to wander across the plains with their flocks of sheep, living in tents in a way that has hardly changed in hundreds of years.

The weather-beaten face of an Uzbeki man reveals all the ruggedness characteristic of his race. The Uzbekis are a Turkic people who came together as a nation probably around the 15th century.

A rich republic

Thanks to its fertile oases, good pastures and dry continental climate, Uzbekistan is one of the richest agricultural areas in the old Soviet Union. Its affluence naturally caused envy in other parts of the country, particularly where there were food shortages. In Moscow, for example, the word 'Uzbek' is freely used as an insult. Never famed for their modesty or tact, the

Uzbeks are proud to claim that their country could feed 100 million people. With a fast-growing population of around 20 million, this may yet turn out to be necessary.

The republic has rich reserves of coal, natural gas and petroleum. Several metallic ores are mined, including gold in the Kyzylkum desert. Uzbekistan is one of the world's largest cotton producers. Its industries include food-processing, chemicals and heavy machinery. Cattle and sheep-breeding also play their part in the nation's economic success-story.

The capital, Tashkent, has suffered the same fate as Ashkhabad: much of this ancient city was destroyed by an earthquake in 1966 which made 300,000 people homeless. Extensively rebuilt in a variety of styles – the brochures accurately describe it as 'a museum of Soviet architecture' – Tashkent has some good public buildings, museums and parks, wide boulevards, and, of course, the inevitable high-rise apartment blocks. In the old town a few 15th- and 16th-century buildings have survived. The Barak-Khana Medrese, a 16th-century theological school, is the headquarters of the Islamic religion in Central Asia. Nearby is a beautifully decorated library containing several antique Korans. But

A fruit and vegetable market in Bukhara, formerly a focal point in the caravan trade between Europe and Asia, and still an important trading centre for farmers and nomads from the neighbouring desert.

visitors to Uzbekistan rarely stay long in Tashkent. The ancient cities of Bukhara, Khiva and Samarkand make more pressing demands on their attention.

Khiva is chiefly remarkable as a complete architectural ensemble, its finest buildings erected in either the 16th or the 19th century – the two great periods of the city's glory. A walk around the old town is like stepping into the Thousand and One Nights, with its palaces, harems, mosques and minarets. At the Medrese of Allaluli Khan is a museum dedicated to Avicenna, the great 11th-century Persian philosopher-scientist whose *Canon of Medicine* has been described as 'the most famous single book in the history of medicine in both East and West'.

Samarkand is better known to English travellers, if only because of shadowy memories of a once-famous book of poems by James Elroy Flecker called *The Golden Journey to Samarkand*. It is one of the great cities of history, as well as one of the oldest. It was successively conquered by Alexander the Great (329 BC), Genghiz Khan (who destroyed it in 1220), and Timur – or Tamerlane. Timur made it his imperial capital in 1370 and rebuilt it magnificently. Among the

many unforgettable sights in this 'Rome of the Orient' is the Street of Tombs, containing mosques and mausoleums of Timur's family; Registan Square, with its historic theological colleges dating from the 15th to the 17th centuries; and the throne and tomb of Timur himself in the Gur Emir Mausoleum. In their combinations of daring forms and striking exterior decoration – coloured domes and tiles in turquoise, cobalt, yellow and green, the use of marble, mosaics and gold – these buildings reach a standard of perfection not easily matched anywhere in the world.

Bukhara was founded in the 1st century AD, and by the time of the Arab invasion in the 8th century was a thriving centre of trade and manufacture. In the 9th and 10th centuries it was the capital of the Persian Samanid dynasty, renowned for its exquisite pottery and brick architecture, as well as for its literature. In 1220 the city fell to Genghiz Khan, and in 1370 to Tamerlane.

Uzbekistan is one of the biggest producers of both raw and finished cotton in the world, so there are plenty of patterned cotton fabrics to choose from at this market stall in Samarkand.

One of several embroidery schools in Bukhara, each with its own special techniques and variants of this ancient art. All the embroidery is done by hand, and only by women.

Bukhara's greatest period was in the 16th century, when it became the capital of an immense Khanate under the Shaybanid dynasty. The Russians established a protectorate here in 1868.

Bukhara has virtually year-round sunshine. The city used up so much water from the river Zeravshan that this former tributary of the Amu Darya now dries up in the desert sands long before it reaches its goal.

Many of Bukhara's historic monuments and streets have survived to be admired today. As a 1981 Soviet brochure puts it with unusual generosity: 'Bukhara has continued to live its own life in spite of a succession of powers ... The covered bazaars, the walls and doorways, the caravenserais, the elegant minarets decorated with

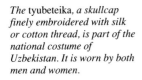

The tyubeteika, *a skullcap finely embroidered with silk or cotton thread, is part of the national costume of Uzbekistan. It is worn by both men and women.*

arabesques, the domes and majestic arches, are the guardians of a people's soul ...'

Bukhara has many fine mosques, in particular the huge Kalyan mosque with its enormous dome, and a 12th-century minaret that can be climbed for a stunning view over the city. There are also several *medreses* (theological schools), one of which, the beautifully-decorated Mir-Arab, is still functioning. The Mausoleum of Ismail Samani, dedicated in the late 9th century to the founder of the Samanid dynasty, lies at one end of Kirov park. This simple yet breathtaking

building – basically a cube surmounted by a dome, and made entirely of brick – subtly changes its appearance as the sun moves round it during the course of the day.

Mountain lands

The same conviction, even more strongly and fiercely held, can be found in the two mountainous republics that form the extreme south of the old Soviet Union: Kyrgyzstan and Tajikistan.

There are numerous music and dance groups in Uzbekistan, most of them amateurs. Some turn professional, however, and provide ethnic entertainment in theatres and night-clubs throughout what used to be the Soviet Union.

The balalaika is a three-stringed instrument of the lute family. It is surprisingly versatile, coming in six sizes from piccolo to double bass. Records published on the Soviet Melodiya label give a good idea of the instrument's range.

More than half the territory of Tajikistan lies above 10,000 feet, its highest peak being Mount Pamir at 24,589 feet. Ski resorts are being developed, but the country is of particular interest to serious hunters, naturalists and mountaineers. Topography and climate are both varied and there is a consequent wealth of plant and animal life: at least 5000 species of flowers, brown bears, wild goats, golden eagles and snakes in the mountains; lizards, gophers and jerboas in the deserts; and Bukhara deer in the forests.

Dushanbe, the capital, is a modern city with a name meaning 'Monday' – the day when markets were held there. The Muslim Tajiks are closely related to the Persians by race and language. Their love of bold, bright colours, often jumbled together in striking profusion, is said to be inspired by the dazzling springtime flowers in their mountain meadows.

Kyrgyzstan is also a country of magnificent mountain ranges with high jagged peaks, fertile valleys and areas of dense forest. Here too the animal life is rich, with wild pigs, brown bears, grey wolves, lynx, deer and goats. The Kyrgyz still go hunting with golden eagles on their wrists, and play a game called Ulak-Tartysh which involves throwing, catching and wrestling for a live goat while mounted on horseback. Needless to say they are impressive horsemen. Their equestrian skills, and the fine horses they breed, can be admired at the racecourse in the capital, Bishkek (known until 1991 as Frunze). Fermented mare's milk, or *kumyss*, is traditionally offered to visitors; but as one seasoned Soviet traveller, the *Guardian*'s former Moscow correspondent Martin Walker, advises: 'Breathe through your mouth and just swallow – it smells worse than it tastes, and it is very good for your stomach. Be warned that it is slightly fizzy.'

Kazakhstan, Soviet showpiece

Kazakhstan is, after Russia, the second largest republic in the old USSR, with 16 million inhabitants living in an area more than five times the size of France and four times that of Ukraine. The country has been so thoroughly colonised that the Kazakhs are actually a minority – numbering only 6 million. They live mostly on the steppe, despite its torrid summers and icy winters, raising sheep; they leave the capital, Alma-Ata, to the multitude of Ukrainian and Russian immigrants.

Because of its vast, thinly-populated steppes, Kazakhstan was chosen as the site for the nuclear weapons testing centre at Sernipalatinsk and for the Cosmodrome at Baikonur, where the world's first manned space flight was launched. It was here, too, that the Virgin Lands Scheme was developed – the creation in the mid-1950s of farmland out of uncultivated steppes. This was largely the brainchild of Khrushchev, whose reputation soared with its apparent success, then plummeted as the intensive monoculture of wheat led to soil exhaustion and erosion, and to the humiliation of having to import grain from the United States. In the long term the scheme worked well, as more balanced agricultural techniques were applied, although this success came too late to save Khrushchev, who was ousted from power in October 1964.

A tea-house in Dushanbe, capital of the Central Asian republic of Tajikistan. Such places are cool, pleasant and relaxing, offering shelter from the sun and the sand-laden wind. In the Islamic tradition, they are frequented only by men, who spend hours here chatting and drinking the refreshing black or green tea.

The Kingdom of Nature

Tundra, taïga and steppe: these are three words that Russia has given to the geography of the world. They evoke images of immense plains, of a wild, sometimes hostile grandeur, of flat 360-degree horizons and of grey light: in sum, the beauty of unspoilt nature. But this is only half the story. The other half consists of progress, modernisation and huge industrial combines.

Farthest north is the flat, almost barren tundra zone, with its permanently frozen subsoil. Here the cold earth and the fierce winds allow only stunted, tortured-looking vegetation to grow: grasses, mosses, lichens, dwarf birches and willows that are more like bushes than trees. Nothing grows higher than a yard from the ground. During the brief two-month summer, before the September snowfalls, the tundra explodes into colour. On the slightest rocky outcrop, in the thinnest layer of soil, the flowers seem to celebrate their revenge on winter. They multiply across the ground, so short as to be almost indistinguishable from the mosses and lichens, then blossom into vast bright carpets of yellow, white or red – a fantastic sight from the air. Some of these flowers are actually dwarf trees – bonsai created by the tundra with all their features scaled down in perfect proportion. Yet so dazzling is the display of colour that to find one of these trees, say a willow six inches high, complete with tiny leaves, you have to look extremely closely.

To appreciate the colours of the taiga – a huge forest zone south of the tundra, stretching from west to east and covering millions of square miles – you must come in autumn. On one particular night, the temperature will suddenly fall far below zero. At a stroke, summer has gone, and the leaves of maples and birches turn to blazing reds and golds that thrill the soul and make our autumn colours seem pale and watery by comparison. It is the sudden cold that does it. Viewed from an aeroplane or a hilltop, the deciduous forests appear like a sea of raging flame among the evergreen pines. They eclipse even the gaily-painted *izby* – the log cabins that dot the Russian countryside – making their strident colours seem dull. The Russians compare the autumn in the taiga to the dying flames of a woman's beauty. They call it *bab'ye lyeto* – 'old woman's summer'. It is certainly the most spectacular autumn in the world.

South of the taiga is the steppe. This consists of a northern, relatively narrow belt of forest, and a wider belt of grassy plains extending right across Ukraine and Russia, east into Siberia and south into Kazakhstan. On

The River Amur which, together with the Ussuri, marks the border between China and south-eastern Siberia. Fed by abundant rainfall and frozen for only one or two months in winter, it is a busy waterway for most of the year, with merchant ships and barges carrying coal, grain and ore.

these plains, the grasses are sometimes tall enough to hide a man, even a man on horseback, and you can approach the wildest animals without seeing them or being seen. The word 'steppe' is probably the most evocative of those three geographical names, prompting images of open, monotonous landscapes. For Russians, though, it has a special emotional significance, just as the word 'sea' has for the people of Britain.

The importance of the natural world was not underestimated by Communism. Here is a short passage from Professor Laptev's book *Man and Nature*, (Progress Editions, Moscow, 1979): 'For Man and in

The harfang *or Great Snowy Owl, whose plumage changes colour with the seasons, is a protected species in Russia.*

The Siberian lynx is another protected species. These beautiful animals are small and graceful, weighing no more than 90lbs. A popular adventure film about the life of a national park warden, Kunak, has made the Siberian lynx a favourite among Russian children.

The Siberian tiger is in serious danger of extinction, with only a few hundred left in the wild. They resemble the Indian tiger apart from their longer fur, which is also somewhat paler and softer.

Astrakhan is made from the fleeces of young karakul *lambs. Their wool grows in tight curls which loosen as they grow older, which means that in order to obtain the finest astrakhan fleeces the lambs are killed when only a few days old.*

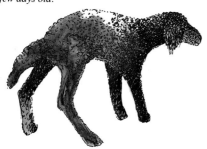

the name of Man, Socialist society safeguards and restores Nature and its beauty. Multiple bonds link Man's health, his psychic state and ability to work, with his environment. Nature is so important for the satisfaction of Man's spiritual needs, for his entire well-being, that it must have a place at the centre of the Socialist state.'

Laptev's book is filled with quotations from Marx, Engels and Lenin, including detailed provisions from the first Soviet constitution for the protection of nature. Yet no amount of fine words can disguise the fact that the record of Communism in matters of pollution and ecological destruction has been every bit as bad as that of capitalism, and in many areas much worse. The sheer vastness of the Soviet Union has, of course, kept certain habitats out of man's reach, and in recent years public opinion – in the form of journals and associations – has sprung to the defence of the country's natural heritage: with some success, it should be said. Ecological movements are now very forceful, and well represented on elected bodies both in Moscow and the republics. A number of bad practices have been stopped (such as the pollution of Lake Baikal) and foolish or risky projects (such as reversing the flow of certain Siberian rivers) nipped in the bud. Soviet man, having lost touch with nature in the great thrust for industrialisation, is now doing his best to repair the damage.

A patch of ground

On the great wheat plains of Ukraine the tractors and combine-harvesters have advanced in ranks across the fields and re-drawn an entire landscape. The scene resembles a propaganda film, full of heroic production statistics, proudly recounting the agricultural triumphs of socialism. Nature here is no more than a tool for the use of man, or a huge open-air factory whose workers live in towns or ugly concrete villages.

Under the Soviet system of agriculture, now famed more for its inefficiency and waste than for any positive achievements, there were two types of farm: the *sovkhoz*, or state farm, in which the workers were paid wages; and the *kolkhoz*, or collective farm, where there were quotas of production and delivery to be met, but the farmers decided collectively how to meet them. The average *sovkhoz* had about 800 workers living in settlements grouped around the central farm complex where machinery, fuel and supplies were kept. One or two shops, the secondary school and clinic were also located centrally, with primary schools in the

surrounding settlements. The *kolkhoz* was similarly arranged around a main farmstead in the largest or most conveniently-situated village.

The system, imposed by Stalin in the late 1920s, was not a success. By the time of Stalin's death in 1953, agricultural production in the Soviet Union was in many areas actually lower than it had been in the last years of the Tsars. Yet even after Khrushchev came to power, the authorities failed to see that they were forcing people to work against their own interests, and continued to run counter-productive campaigns such as Khrushchev's crackdown on private ownership of cows. Peasants were forced to hand over their animals to collective farms, with the result that milk production fell. The essence of the problem was pinpointed by Abramov in his short story, *The New Life* (1963): 'For his work-day a peasant would get ten per cent of the collective hay he gathered ... So a peasant had to gather enough hay for at least eight or nine cows in order to look after his own....'

The only real success came from a concession in the system. Both state farm-workers and collective farmers were allowed small plots of land to cultivate for private use. In the late 1970s it was estimated that these private plots produced between 20 and 25 per cent of food consumed in the USSR, even though they occupied only 3 per cent of the nation's cultivated land.

Following new legislation in the 1980s which allowed farmers greater control of the land, and freed

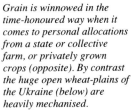

Grain is winnowed in the time-honoured way when it comes to personal allocations from a state or collective farm, or privately grown crops (opposite). By contrast the huge open wheat-plains of the Ukraine (below) are heavily mechanised.

all types of agricultural units from restrictions on their use, the Soviet Union stopped creating state farms. Some were broken up to make way for new collective farms. But, in the end, it was the success of the little individual plots of land that pointed the way forward.

These even became fashionable in the cities. Companies and agencies would offer their workers a small garden in the suburbs as a bonus. This might be anything up to a quarter of an acre in area, and workers were allowed to build a shed or even a small *izba*.The only condition imposed was that the plot should not be given over entirely to the cultivation of flowers – which are something of an obsession for the Russians.

This was a straightforward reversal of earlier policy, when the 'individual plot' – even if legal – was condemned in state propaganda as 'petit bourgeois'.

This change of policy caused much amusement in the eastern and southern republics of the Union, where the individual plot had long been recognised as the bedrock of whatever prosperity they had.

By the late 1980s there was a full-blown craze for these plots right across the western republics, and even the cereal-growing plains of Ukraine were dotted with mini-*izbas* with wooden fences, behind which were vegetables and fruit bushes, chickens, rabbits, even pigs and cows – now officially allowed again.

In his highly successful novel *Matushka*, published in 1984, the Siberian writer Valentin Rasputin describes with obvious relish how an old country woman looks lovingly after her cow, keeping her in prime condition, spruce and neat, and sparing no effort to find her the best grass. The novel is a barely disguised hymn to individualism and enterprise – the new realities of a Soviet Union undergoing radical change.

The mysteries of the samovar

Growing your own vegetables and raising a little livestock on the side – indeed, the whole culture of the 'individual plot' – are part of a revival of traditional ways of life that has swept the territories of the former Soviet Union. And there are few more potent symbols of the traditional past than the *samovar* – the Russian equivalent of the kettle on the hob.

In city flats you will see electric *samovars*, but the countryside is the place to look for the real thing, in the gaily painted *izbas* of rural settlements. Here the *samovar* has pride of place, a gleaming copper cylinder often with the word 'Tula' (the name of the town where it was manufactured) still half-legible on the side.

Market day in Vilnius, capital of Lithuania. A stallholder laboriously unwraps some eggs which the shopper carries loose in a bag, rather than in a box.

Sunflowers are an important crop in the republics of the former Soviet Union. Their leaves are used for cattle fodder and the seeds pressed to make oil.

Another market day draws to an end; the economically hard-pressed peasants sell their produce in an ironic setting: in front of doors whose decoration represents the supposed plenty of Soviet agriculture.

Haymaking in southern Siberia. Note the 1930s vintage pick-up truck, battered, one-eyed, but still viable in an economy where no-one can afford to throw anything away.

An entire ceremony accompanies the making of tea: glowing coals gently heat the water inside the *samovar*, which in turn heats a tiny white porcelain teapot perched on top. Inside the teapot is a concentrated infusion of tea, dense, jet-black and fragrant. The *babushka* religiously pours a little of this dark, smoking brew into the cup and dilutes it with water from the *samovar*, strong or weak according to each person's taste. To cool the boiling liquid, tea-lovers pour it into the saucer and gingerly take a few sips. Again, this is not something that you will see in cities any more, although it persists among country folk.

Apart from the *samovar*, the interior of the *izba* is sparsely furnished. This is not necessarily due to poverty, but is more a matter of custom. Rugs provide the main decoration, and are sometimes hung on the walls as well as laid on the floor. Fine sideboards and dressers, painted chests of drawers and huge wardrobes

Folk costume, still worn by older peasants, outside an izba *near the town of . Vladimir in western Russia.*

are found only in the Baltic states of Latvia, Estonia and Lithuania, or in the western parts of Belorussia.

The stove is an essential item in the Russian *izba*. These are made of cast iron or stoneware and are always fat, to give off the necessary heat for the severe Russian winter. To Western visitors, used to their brick houses, it is often a surprise to see how warm an *izba* can be. Despite their often ramshackle and whimsical appearance, and an occasional tilt due to shifting foundations, they make a remarkably good job of keeping out the cold. It has to be said that Russians are, by and large, less sensitive to cold than people from milder climates.

It would be a mistake to imagine life in the countryside as idyllic. Despite its beauty, the Russian winter is a difficult time for man and beast. In some parts of northern Siberia, winter continues practically the whole year round, and what summer there is does not last long enough to grow crops of any kind. And

The interior of a Russian country izba, with its massive wooden bed, unadorned timber walls and double-thickness duvets.

The Kyrgyz people of Central Asia have a particular fondness for multi-coloured quilts and cushions. The Kyrgyz have preserved an exceptional number of their old tastes and traditions.

A gathering of friends in Kyrgyzstan (far right), close to the borders of China and India. Interiors are often tent-like and padded with bright materials.

yet, in defiance of nature, people put up huge greenhouses with entire gardens inside them, where fruit and vegetables can be grown. There is even some talk of building whole villages under glass – like something out of one of the science-fiction stories which Russians read so keenly.

However harsh the winters, summer brings its compensations and gaiety – in hundreds of different forms across this sprawling land. One thinks, for instance, of Kyrgyz shepherds who spend the hot months living in tents with their wives and children, while their flocks graze around them in the high mountain pastures; of the very different shepherd-horsemen of the Volga; of the lumberjacks of Baikal and Amur; of the workers on immense projects such as the 2,800-mile gas pipeline from Siberia to Ukraine; or the new branch of the Trans-Siberian Railway, the Baikal-Amur Magistral or BAM: heroic schemes that are almost unimaginable to the inhabitants of much smaller countries like our own.

Casualties of the BAM

The BAM starts at Ust Kut, to the north of Lake Baikal, and runs eastward for 2000 miles to Komsomolsk-na-Amure, from where it connects again with the main Trans-Siberian line at Khabarovsk. Its purpose is to serve the new industries in eastern Siberia and the Far East, but another probable reason for its construction was to provide a back-up line north of the main Trans-Siberian which runs uncomfortably close to the Chinese border.

So fraught with setbacks was this project that it took a full five years from the date of its inauguration in

1984 to the time when it entered service. Apart from problems of poor workmanship and morale, there were also daunting natural obstacles to overcome: seven mountain ranges to cross, tunnels to excavate through frozen soil, and over 3000 bridges to build across rivers that were solid ice for much of the time. Nor were the weather conditions exactly favourable: with winter lasting for ten months of the year at temperatures as low as -62°C; and summer, when it came, bringing swarms of mosquitoes and heatwaves that suddenly revealed marshes, rivers, and even forests that had previously lain hidden beneath a blanket of thick snow. As if the region were not already unwelcoming enough, most of it also lay in an earthquake zone.

On either side of the track, along the great scar it has ploughed across the landscape, lie the casualties of the BAM – scores of broken-down bulldozers, lorries, diggers and cranes, worn out by the impossible conditions and abandoned like smashed toys. Long-completed stations and other railway installations have already begun to fall apart under the extreme onslaught of the weather.

During the building of the BAM, the gangs of workmen lived on special trains that moved forward with the railhead and the track-laying machinery. They slept in dormitory-wagons fitted with individual cubicles. They ate in canteen-wagons, relaxed in saloon-wagons, and changed into and out of their heavy working clothes in a changing-room wagon. When they were ill they went to the infirmary-wagon. In severe weather, supplies of food could not always be guaranteed and the work-gangs were issued with rifles in order to shoot bears and wolves for meat in case of need. Most of the workmen quit the job as soon as they had completed their one-year contracts, defeated by the

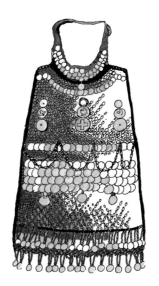

Elaborate necklaces hung with gold and silver coins are often worn by the women of Central Asia. Mothers hand them down to their daughters, but also teach them the craft of making them.

In tea-houses or chaikhana *like this one in the Kyrgyz capital of Bishkek (or Pishpek), tea is drunk green and occasionally spiced with cinnamon. The clientele is exclusively male.*

cold and hardship. Some, though, stayed for several years, as if bewitched by nature's pitilessness, savagery and awe-inspiring superiority to man.

A feeling for nature

Whether one thinks of those stubborn-hearted workers on the BAM or the *kolkhoz* farmers lovingly tending their allotments from Ukraine to Armenia, there is a restless urge throughout the entire territory of the old Soviet Union to improve, to construct, and to wring the best from the natural environment. But there is also

A Ukrainian girl with flower-decked hair and an embroidered blouse graces a country festival. Most of the traditional festivals survived the Soviet decades.

something deeper: a desire to return to nature, whether as ally or opponent, and to link up with the traditions and culture of previous times. This is why an author like Valentin Rasputin is so widely read, because he expresses this impulse for an entire generation. It is worth quoting a passage at length from his novel *Farewell to Matyora*, about a village on a river island which is to be flooded following the construction of a new hydroelectric dam. Here he describes the island through the eyes of an old woman:

'From where she stood, on the highest point of the island, she could see everything as if it lay in the palm of her hand: the Angara river in the distance, and her own Matyora beyond the pine wood. The island stretched almost as far as the horizon, separated from it only by a slender line of water that shone at its furthest edge. The right arm of the river snaked away in a series of sharp bends, growing steadily narrower as it went. The left arm, nearer and calmer, seemed suspended from its steep bank, forming part of Matyora, still and tranquil at this hour, under a feeble sun. That was why they called it "our Angara" in Matyora.

'The river was the centre of the village: it was there that they launched their boats; it was there that they drew their water; and it was there that the village children began their discovery of the world. Everything, down to the smallest pebble, was learned and retained there.

'The island stretched out peacefully, all the more dear to her for its precise territorial limits: beyond lay not an expanse of dry land, but water. From one end to the other, one shore to the other, it contained enough space, wealth, beauty and wild places, enough pairs of creatures of every species – a sufficiency of everything. Never mind that it was cut off from the continent. It lay full length below her, tranquil and secret, gorged with the juices and saps of a summer that had come early.

'To the right of the knoll where Daria sat, the autumn wheat grew dense and green. Behind it rose the forest, still rather colourless, not fully in leaf, with dark patches marking the clumps of pines and firs. Through it, from top to bottom, ran the road to Podgoma.

'Near the woods, to the left of the road, lay a pasture, closed on two sides, open to the village and "our Angara" on the others. There were cows grazing there; she could hear one of their bells tinkling sweetly. And there, like the king of trees, stood an ancient larch, decapitated by a lightning-stroke but still immense, at least fifty feet high, with thick branches growing wide of the trunk. Not far from the "king of trees" grew a birch, looking as if it had wanted to approach its sovereign but had given up the attempt, frightened at the larch's terrible aspect or petrified by its lordly scorn.'

Secret gardens

The island in Rasputin's story has a meaning that goes far beyond the Siberian context. It is an island in the heart of the troubled Soviet soul, a refuge, a place of return, a secret garden of the spirit, menaced by the greedy and interfering materialism of the modern age.

Moldavian costume. Moldavians are ethnically and linguistically Romanian, and their land, in the extreme south-west of the old Soviet Union, is divided between the states of Romania and the republic of Moldova.

A scene of everyday life in Lithuania. Even in such advanced, westernised republics, the horse still has a place in agricultural life.

Everywhere people are building their islands, in their suburban gardens, in the countryside, growing vegetables and flowers and putting up odd-shaped *izbas* where they can spend their week-ends away from the concrete and fumes of their everyday lives.

This is a familiar feeling all over the developed world, linked to the enormous growth of environmental consciousness. Yet almost fifty years ago, socialists such as George Orwell, author of *Animal Farm* and *Nineteen Eighty-Four*, were already warning of the dangers of ignoring nature in the relentless pursuit of an ideal society. In his 1946 essay 'Some Thoughts on the Common Toad', he asked: 'If we kill all pleasure in the actual process of life, what sort of future are we preparing for ourselves? If a man cannot enjoy the return of spring, why should he be happy in a labour-saving Utopia? What will he do with the leisure that the machine will give him?.... By preaching the doctrine that nothing is to be admired except steel and concrete, one merely makes it a little surer that human beings will have no outlet for their surplus energy except in hatred and leader worship.' Prophetic words, and not just for the Soviet Union.

about cars, which are still the exception rather than the rule in rural areas. Apart from the main arteries, the roads are frequently little better than tracks. In some remote corners there are more men on horseback than behind the wheels of cars. And in many parts of the East and South-East of the old Soviet Union the horse is still the most practical means of transport.

Another favourite means of 'getting back to nature' is provided by canoes and kayaks. Increasing numbers of holidaymakers are taking to the rivers, where they spend two or three weeks drifting downstream, living off the fish and game which they catch or shoot themselves.

The question of water

Mention of rivers brings us to the single greatest environmental issue in the former Soviet Union: water. Both pollution and supply present urgent problems that have consequences not just for the people of Russia and its allied republics but for the whole world.

At the heart of the problem is the River Volga, the principal waterway of the former Soviet Union, the longest river in Europe, and a symbol of Russia, featuring strongly in folklore and popular song. A quarter of the population of the former USSR live in its basin, which occupies about a third of the territory of

The Trans-Siberian Railway was begun in 1891 and completed in 1915. It takes ten days to travel the 5,776 miles from Moscow to Vladivostok, which is also one of the busiest freight routes in the world.

One really needs to spend a few days and nights in one of these *izbas* to get to know the sort of life people lead there. In the autumn they pick mushrooms and berries of every kind, supplies of which appear to be inexhaustible even on the outskirts of cities. Sometimes they help themselves surreptitiously to a few potatoes from a *kolkhoz*, remembering of course to replace the plants carefully once the petty theft has been committed – although they often find that the plant has already been plundered by someone else, so widespread is the practice! Such are the minor sins against socialism....

Those who have neither *izba* nor *dacha* set off on foot across the taiga with rucksacks on their backs to savour the joys of the open air, camping rough, living the simple life. They catch whatever train happens to be running, get off at a station that takes their fancy, and put up their tents somewhere along a quiet road in the backwoods.

They are lucky in not having to worry too much

European Russia, Ukraine, and Belorussia – more than half a million square miles. Known as Volga Matushka, 'Mother Volga', it rises in the Valdai Hills north-west of Moscow, and flows in a huge sickle-shaped curve, first south-east, then south-west, for a total of 2,193 miles, and enters the Caspian Sea at Astrakhan. Its economic importance is enormous, for it carries, with its main tributaries the Oka and the Kama, over half the passenger traffic and around two-thirds of the freight traffic of the entire CIS waterway system. Through a network of navigation canals, the Volga is connected to the Baltic sea, the Moskva and Don rivers, and the Sea of Azov. The Volga is also one of the biggest sources of hydroelectric power in the CIS with dams and reservoirs at Rybinsk, Saratov, Kuibyshev (now Samara) and Volgograd. Other reservoirs supply cities, industries and irrigation systems right along its course.

This is all very impressive, but the huge volume of water tapped off along the way has led to a gradual fall in the level of the Caspian Sea over recent decades. With its low rainfall and high evaporation rate, the Caspian relies heavily on its supply from the Volga, even though it is also fed by the smaller Ural and Terek rivers from the north. Ecologists have campaigned hard and with some success for the introduction of stricter controls on pollution in the Caspian Sea, the closure of several particularly damaging factories, and the

scrapping of numerous plans to build yet more dams and canals. Fortunately, the water level in the Caspian has started rising again, bringing life back to sections of the Volga delta that had dried up: good news for the troubled caviar industry, for these are ideal waters for the sturgeon.

The problems of the Caspian pale into insignificance compared with those of the Aral Sea. This has been an outright ecological disaster. The Aral Sea, located to the east of the Caspian in South Central Asia, was formerly the fourth largest body of inland water in the world. A salt-water lake that supported a large fishing industry, it lost 60 per cent of its volume and sank to little more than half its original depth between 1960 and the late 1980s. The fishing ports of Aralsk in the north-east and Muynak in the south were now miles from the water. The reason for this was the extraction for agricultural irrigation of immense quantities of water from the two great rivers that flowed into the Aral Sea: the Amu Darya from the south, which no longer has the force even to reach the Aral, and the Syr Darya from the north-east. Together these rivers accounted for about 80 per cent of inflow to the sea, and, since evaporation took out almost as much water annually as the rivers supplied, disaster was inevitable. The vastly increased salt and mineral content of the water made it unfit for

A country halt on the Trans-Siberian Railway. Tempting as it is to jump off and look around, the train stops only for a minute at these stations, although you get longer at cities such as Irkutsk.

The monotony of the menus in the Trans-Siberian dining car is relieved by offers of fresh food from peasants who climb onto the train at country stations. The woman here is offering freshly laid eggs.

human use and unsuitable for the fish that once swam there. The fishing industry – based on sturgeon, carp, barbel and roach – is now in ruins, and increased soil salinity is threatening crops.

In the meantime, the republics that received the water from the Aral's two feed rivers – Uzbekistan, Turkmenistan and Kazakhstan – and were able to convert huge areas of previously barren terrain into farmland, started to demand more water, and made common cause in their appeals to Moscow for a solution to their problems of water shortages.

A scheme was produced to reverse the flow of two great Siberian rivers, the Ob and Yenisey, and divert their waters southwards to irrigate the deserts of Central Asia. Scientists have argued that this would reduce the supply of fresh water into the Arctic and lead to the ice-cap creeping hundreds of miles south into Siberia, with disastrous consequences for the environment. The debate goes back to the days of Brezhnev, who was in favour of the flow-reversal scheme. Many journalists, historians, scientists, lawyers and writers opposed it, and kept the argument raging for several years, notably

through the 'Nature' pages of the weekly *Literaturnaya Gazeta*, published by the Soviet Writers' Union. One of the scheme's opponents was Dr Abel Aganbegyan, who later became one of President Gorbachev's leading economic advisers. Public opinion eventually forced Gorbachev to drop the scheme in 1987, soon after coming to power, but calls for it to be reconsidered have persisted. These have come particularly from the Central Asian republics, highlighting a clash of interests between their fast-growing Muslim populations and the Russian north. It is to be hoped that in the reorganisation of political life and economic priorities in the new Commonwealth of Independent States the lessons of the disaster in the Aral Sea will be taken to heart, and such large-scale tampering with nature's balance will no longer be considered worth the terrible ecological risks involved.

A spot of caviar

When the water level of the Caspian Sea dropped, the worst effects were felt by the caviar industry. This depends on the 20,000 tons of sturgeon that are caught in the spring and summer of each year as they swim upstream from the mouth of the Volga to their spawning grounds. From this quantity of fish, the canning factories, located between Astrakhan and the sea, will extract around 2000 tons of roe to make one of the world's most sought-after delicacies: caviar.

Left to themselves – which they scarcely ever are today – sturgeons can grow to an enormous age and size – the Great or Beluga Sturgeon, which is the largest, lives as long as 100 years; an adult measures 28 feet in length, and weighs well over one and a quarter tons. They live off small fishes and invertebrates but have even been known to eat young Caspian seals. Female sturgeons are sexually mature at 15 years of age, when they produce an enormous number of eggs – up to 7.7 million at a time – and it is this roe, preserved in salt (which also brings out the flavour) that makes caviar. It may be pasteurised, or if not, very carefully stored at between 0°C and -7°C. Beluga caviar is black or grey, osetrina is grey, grey-green or brown, and sevruga is greenish black. The

Kyrgyz shepherds, famed for their horsemanship, tend their flocks in a national park, where ancient pastoral methods are encouraged as part of the nation's heritage.

Hunting with birds of prey, including falcons and eagles, is still widely practised in the high mountain republic of Kyrgyzstan.

most valuable of all is golden caviar, from the much smaller sterlet, an exclusively freshwater fish which grows to only about a yard in length and lays less than 150,000 eggs.

Nearly all genuine caviar comes from the former USSR or Iran, but there are substitutes which are sometimes labelled 'caviar', such as the red roes of salmon, or lumpfish and whitefish roes dyed black with ink taken from cuttlefish. If water pollution, damming of rivers and overfishing continue to take their toll on the population of sturgeon, real caviar may well become an even greater rarity.

Along the Volga

For a journey up the Volga there is a choice of several hydrofoils and boats, some of them floating luxury hotels. The river is navigable for 2000 miles, and the journey is fascinating. It begins in the delta region, between the Caspian Sea and Astrakhan, among rice-paddies and pastures, where shepherds guard their flocks of *karakul* sheep; it is from these newborn lambs that the fur-like Astrakhan fleeces are taken to make luxurious hats and collars for coats. The river here is broad and slow, and looks and feels like the sea, with large freighters and passenger vessels coming and going

A street market in Och, Kyrgyzstan, where the people have a distinctly Mongolian look. Unlike the tea-houses, markets are frequented largely by women.

across the wide waters. Soon, though, you come to Astrakhan, a busy port with a large fishing fleet, canning industries and shipyards, but also a fine cathedral and 16th-century *kremlin* (castle) standing among its many waterways and bridges.

Fifteen hours upstream you come to the Volgograd dam. To the left is the gigantic triumphal arch marking the entry to the 60-mile Volga-Don Ship Canal, built between 1948 and 1952 to connect these two great Russian rivers. Immediately to the north stands the city of Volgograd, perhaps better known to the world as Stalingrad. (It was originally named Tsaritsyn, becoming Stalingrad in 1925, and Volgograd in 1961.)

It was here, between September 15, 1942 and February 2, 1943, that one of the decisive battles of the Second World War took place, as a German army of over 400,000 men attempted to capture the city and was then encircled by the Russians. The Germans inflicted terrible destruction on the city but were then pinned down and isolated with dwindling supplies through the months of December and January.

After losing three-quarters of their troops, the Germans finally capitulated. 'This crushing disaster to the German army,' wrote Winston Churchill in his *History of the Second World War*, 'ended Hitler's prodigious effort to conquer Russia by force of arms.' The final cost of the battle was almost a million lives.

The city was restored from its ruins and now thrives again, with much heavy industry and a rich cultural life. On Mamayev Hill, overlooking the majestic sweep of the Volga, stands a great monumental park in memory of the war dead, with towering statues carved in the Soviet-heroic style – which manage to be tragic and moving despite the Superman muscles and inevitable lantern jaws.

The journey upstream continues. Sometimes the river rolls powerfully along, sometimes – where it has been dammed – it is more like a sea. You can still see the old towpaths along the banks where, as recently as a century ago, convicts used to pull the barges by hand. The journey from Astrakhan to Nizhny Novgorod (east of Moscow) used to take two months – a gruelling trip which claimed many convicts' lives.

The river opens out again as you reach the gigantic Kuibyshev reservoir (370 miles long by 15 miles wide). Here, between the Zhiguli hills, the water level was

raised by 60 feet in 1957 when a large hydroelectric dam was built. This now supplies electricity for the Russo-Italian Fiat car factory, set up in 1970 in the nearby city of Togliatti. The city itself, sometimes nicknamed 'Detroit on the Volga', was formerly called Stavropol and situated some distance away, in the depths of what is now the Kuibyshev reservoir. It was named Togliatti in 1964 in honour of the Italian Communist leader, Palmiro Togliatti (1893-1964), who led the Italian party for almost 40 years, and succeeded in making it the biggest Communist party in Western Europe.

The Volga unwinds its landscapes as you pass, caught in a kind of bewitching monotony: from steppe to taiga, the villages succeed one another along the green banks, some colourful, some drab. Every now and then comes a big town, usually with a large dam attached, then that too disappears behind you, and you are into the countryside again.

At the rural landing stages, peasant women come down to the jetty to sell wild berries, cherries, and fruit and vegetables of every kind. Their cheeks are as red as the apples in their baskets, which they insist are grown without chemicals, for natural products are as much in demand here as in the West. The boat stops for half an hour or so, and then moves on.

The villages offer a glimpse of the 'other Russia', leading its own life, cut off even in Soviet times from the great cities of Moscow, Leningrad and Kiev. The village streets are unpaved dirt roads, the shops primitive and homely. Untouched by the fashions of consumer society, life follows a gentler rhythm. Prices are lower too: a comfortable *izba* on the banks of the

Volga, not too isolated and with its own 'central heating' – that is, a big stove – costs the equivalent of two to four months' salary for the average worker. Capitalist speculation in second homes has not yet reached the Volga!

Around Kazan and the confluence of the Volga with the river Kama is Tatar country, mysterious, secretive, yet welcoming too. When a foreigner steps off the boat here it is a major event: the traveller is scrutinised with passionate curiosity. The people here live close to

No fatherland left to defend ... an array of Soviet medals worn by an old soldier from Central Asia.

Infants' cradles on sale in the Kyrgyz town of Och. They may look like souvenirs, but in fact these are still in everyday use.

nature and husband their resources well. They may be poor, but they are the true ecologists, and have more to teach us than we might suspect.

Farther north, at the confluence with the river Oka, comes the city of Gorky, thus named in 1932 after the great short-story writer, playwright and novelist Maxim Gorky who was born there in 1868. It was here that the eminent physicist and human rights campaigner Andrey Sakharov was kept under house-arrest from 1980 to 1986 in an effort to silence him: a measure that was undoubtedly one of the great own goals scored by Soviet propaganda. In October 1990 Gorky reverted to its historic name of Nizhny Novgorod.

Beyond this point the Upper Volga begins, and continues through marshes and forests to its source near Lake Seliger in the Valdai Hills. The river is navigable only in the spring and summer months, after the day in April known as *Ledokhod*, when, with a tremendous exhilarating roar, the waters break free of the ice that has imprisoned them.

Journey's end

The end of your journey approaches. With luck it will have been full of adventures, a series of discoveries and surprises that will live in your memory for years to come. It is worth remembering, though, that even in this extraordinary land, adventure does not come programmed in a tourist itinerary. You will not find it in or around the vast hotels built by the Soviets for Western visitors. You have to venture out of the big cities and towns. For much of the Soviet period this was

difficult, but now there are scarcely any limits to the journeys you can make.

In search of nature, you might have travelled to the Caucasus Mountains, where bears, mountain goats, deer and birds of prey abound among the lakes and forests. Or to Murmansk in the Arctic Circle to see reindeer and polar bears. Or to Siberia for the white tigers, snow leopards and elk. The range of fauna in this gigantic territory is unparalleled: wolves, wild horses, fifteen species of gazelles, hyenas, bison, wild goats, pigs and sheep, walruses, lynx, mink, tortoises, sables, lemmings, polecats, porcupines, jackals ... not to mention almost every species of bird found in Europe and Asia too. On top of all that, the varieties of landscape, and of human inhabitants and their cultures, are equally dizzying.

Variety is the key. For 70 years, we have been accustomed to think of this collection of disparate peoples and environments as one country: the monolithic superpower of the Soviet Union. As we have seen, Lenin and his heirs made almost superhuman efforts to bring them together. Their efforts involved massive experiments with both human nature and the physical world – from the virtual abolition of private property to the damming and diversion of great rivers. We can now see that these experiments were too brutal. Their success existed only in the make-believe world of state propaganda.

Yet even with gentler methods, under Mikhail Gorbachev, the Union proved impossible to hold together. Perhaps, after our journey through just part of its fantastic wealth and diversity, we can begin to understand why.

The republics of the old Soviet Union are some of the heaviest users of timber in the world. Even though they possess one-fifth of the world's forests, the question of re-afforestation will soon become urgent.

Czechoslovakia

The land of the 'velvet revolution' of 1989 has had a chequered history, even by Eastern European standards. In the Middle Ages much of it fell within the kingdom of Bohemia. Then came long centuries as part of the Habsburg Empire, from whose tutelage the Czech Lands (Bohemia and Moravia), along with Slovakia, finally escaped in 1918. Twenty years of freedom after that were followed by Nazi and then Soviet occupation. Now, in spite of all they have been through and accomplished together, the Czechs and Slovaks are preparing to go their separate ways.

A Slovak goatherd in traditional costume drinks goat's milk from a specially carved wooden mug. Such a sight would once have been common in Slovakia, but is now chiefly put on for the benefit of tourists.

Life ambles on at its age-old pace near Zdiar in the Tatra Mountains of eastern Slovakia. Large parts of the region have now been enclosed in a national park, thus helping to preserve its many rare or unique mountain plants.

Previous page:
The Vltava river – or Moldau, in German – at Cesky Krumlov. Southern Bohemia, where the Vltava has its source, is a region of wooded hills and of small lakes and rivers, popular with anglers. The local carp are the most sought-after prize.

Europe's Crossroads

For a country that has existed as an independent state for under three-quarters of a century, Czechoslovakia has accumulated a remarkable number of outstanding dates: 1918 – the year of its creation under the philosopher-president Tomás Masaryk; 1938 – when the leaders of the European powers meeting at Munich handed over parts of it to Hitler, with a full-blown Nazi invasion following the year after; 1948 – the year of the post-war Communist takeover; 1968 – when, in the 'Prague Spring', the party secretary Alexander Dubcek's attempt to establish 'socialism with a human face' was crushed by Soviet tanks ... and finally, 1989 – the 'velvet revolution', the supreme example of 'people power' in Eastern Europe's year of revolutions, when the Communist regime was bloodlessly toppled. This was undoubtedly the greatest year of them all, with fresh hope budding across the country. 'Although small, we were once the spiritual crossroads of Europe,' the new playwright-president Vaclav Havel commented in a New Year's address at the start of 1990. 'Can we not become so again?'

'Crossroads' is an apt description of this long, thin country slicing across the heart of Europe, from the German border in the west to the Ukrainian border in the east. In the Middle Ages its westernmost region, Bohemia, was one of Europe's most powerful kingdoms, and its capital, the 'golden city' of Prague, among the continent's most magnificent. There then followed centuries in which the Czech Lands (Bohemia and Moravia), with Slovakia to the east, were absorbed into the Habsburg Empire centred on Vienna. Even so, the Czechs in particular prospered, and Prague remained one of Europe's great cultural centres. Mozart was a regular visitor in the 18th century, and the 19th and 20th centuries saw an exceptional flowering of native talent, especially in literature and music, with figures such as the novelists Franz Kafka and more recently Milan Kundera and the composers Dvořák, Smetana and Janáček. Slovakia, with its own language and culture remained relatively underdeveloped, but it too was to produce some remarkable people, most notably in recent times Alexander Dubcek. Today it is forming its own increasingly independent-minded republic within the federal Czechoslovak state.

Lakes, plains and a rim of pine-covered mountains are the essential ingredients of the Bohemian landscape. Approaching Czechoslovakia from the west, you first enter the pine forests after leaving Nuremberg in Germany, and they get thicker and more oppressive as you reach the mountain frontier of the Bohemian Forest. Cresting the mountains, you find yourself in a different world. The forests spread out on all sides and, compared with Germany's well-ordered lands the countryside between them is noticeably poorer. Then, as you descend towards the immense plains on the other side, lakes and ponds appear ... hundreds of them. Every village (especially in southern Bohemia) has its stretch of water, often beside the church. Most are artificial, constructed in the Middle Ages for raising carp – still the traditional Christmas dish. The carp are rarer now but the lakes remain, many covered with water weeds. The largest is Lake Rozmberk, extending for nearly 1000 acres. Along with the onion-domed churches, time-blackened statues of the 14th-century local saint John of Nepomuk, stone bridges and gaggles of free-roaming domestic geese, the lakes are an essential part of the old world charm of Bohemian villages.

Baroque is the dominant architectural style throughout this region – even in small village churches

Domestic geese abound throughout Eastern Europe. From Poland to Bulgaria, Bohemia to Russia, they waddle in noisy gaggles along country roads, erratically supervised by urchins armed with switches. For the people of Czechoslovakia, roast goose with knedlíky *(dumplings) is a popular festive dish in winter.*

Forests of pine and birch cover most of the mountain slopes of Slovakia, and until the Second World War timber was the most important local industry. But in recent years, the effect on trees of pollution from neighbouring heavy industrial regions is an increasing threat.

and isolated farmhouses colourwashed in pastel shades of green, pink and blue. The chief glories of towns such as Domazlice, Ceské Budejovice and Telc are their large market squares, bordered imposingly with baroque arcades and narrow, elaborately gabled houses. On their fronts, bas-reliefs in white stucco depict plump cherubs, garlands of flowers or biblical scenes such as Jonah emerging from the whale. Most of the region's original Gothic churches fell prey to the religious wars of the 15th century when, in a foretaste of the Reformation to come, the followers of the reforming priest John Huss defied, and were eventually crushed by, the armed might of Catholic Europe. Many churches were rebuilt in baroque style in the 17th and 18th centuries. Inside, they are gaudily arrayed with gilded, wood-carved angels and brightly daubed saints in striking poses of exhortation. Side aisles sometimes contain a glass coffin with the wax figure of a local bishop, and there is often a statue of a child heavily draped in robes of gold-embroidered velvet – a representation of the famous Infant Jesus of Prague.

On the outskirts of many villages another baroque edifice rises to complete the scene: an 18th-century mansion (often a veritable palace) built by some former noble or princely family in the midst of its huge landed domains. Now it is probably a cultural centre or belongs to a workers' association. Ivy clambers over the mansion's elegant façade, and weeds have long since invaded the terraces and alleys of the park. But still in the neighbouring woods, mossy sandstone statues of hermits and wild beasts recall the romance of past times.

Beyond the baroque finery of the towns and villages, the Bohemian plain spreads out in scarcely noticeable waves from the rocky, forest-covered lands of the west to the alp-like Krkonose Mountains in the north-east –

their pistes in winter a popular weekend playground for Prague's young people. Since the collectivisation of agriculture under the Communists, the plain has largely been given over to cereal crops, and the small, twin-engined aircraft of a local cooperative can sometimes be seen skimming low over the heads of wheat and barley as it sprays them with fertiliser or insecticide. Agriculture is practised on such a large scale here that experts think it will be difficult to return the land to private hands in large enough units to make farming them viable.

East of Bohemia, in Moravia and then in Slovakia, the countryside becomes more rugged and the climate more extreme. The western ranges of the Carpathian

Agricultural workers take a rest in the sun, and in the distance a castle can be seen on the summit of a hill. Under the Communist regime it was the peasants – about 14 per cent of the population – who benefited most, especially in Slovakia where, until the Second World War, most of the land belonged to a few noble families.

Little in this snowbound scene from the Slovak village of Vernár is indicative of the 20th century. The old peasant woman enveloped in the inevitable black, and the cottage walls painted in tints of mauve and brown, are just as they have been for centuries. Only the double-glazed windows offer telltale hints of the modern age.

Mountains dominate Slovakia which is still the country's poorest region. Except in a few industrialised areas, notably around the Slovak capital Bratislava, close to the Austrian and Hungarian borders in the south-west, Slovak life follows many of the ancient patterns. The people are more devoutly Catholic than in the Czech lands. They also make better wines (which can be tasted in the *vinárnen* attached to village cooperatives). Numerous ruined castles, perched impressively on rocky outcrops, bear witness to the troubled centuries when Slovakia was a buffer zone between Christian Europe and the expanding Ottoman Empire, which ended in 1683 with the defeat of the Turks outside Vienna. Higher up, among the mountains

of the Tatra National Park, live the last wild bears in Eastern Europe, as well as eagles and wild sheep. In the narrow valleys between, houses are still built of pine and have dark blue beams and painted floors. And many people still don their traditional costumes for occasions such as weddings.

The ordeal of survival

Under the Communists, the Czechoslovak economy was one of the most successful in Eastern Europe, and its people were among the most prosperous. Even so, conditions were hardly ideal and though the people now

Until the 1950s, the patterns of life in the Orava Valley of north-western Slovakia had scarcely changed for centuries. Since then, even with the industrialisation of parts of the region, some traditional country areas survive.

There are marked differences in the architecture of Czechoslovakia's mountain and lowland regions. In the lowlands, baroque influence is evident everywhere. In the mountains, simple wooden buildings are the rule. Often, as here in the village of Zdiar in Slovakia's High Tatra Mountains, the outsides of houses are brightly painted.

have their freedom life remains in many ways tough. Finding accommodation is the first obsession of every young Czech or Slovak. There are long waiting lists for the state accommodation available in the dreary, concrete, high-rise blocks that surround the country's towns and cities. Officially, people have to wait an average of ten years for a flat; in practice the wait is usually even longer. Consequently, most young couples are obliged to spend several years living with parents or parents-in-law, so it is hardly surprising that the divorce rate is one of the highest in Europe and the birth rate one of the lowest.

There is the option of buying a flat, but you have to be rich to do that. A would-be purchaser has to put down a lump sum of 30,000-60,000 crowns – ten to twenty times the average monthly salary. And saving money is out of the question for people who, even in the professions, scarcely earn enough to see them through to the end of the month. The gradual introduction of a market economy since 1989, though more successful in Czechoslovakia than in many of its formerly Communist neighbours, has sent prices rocketing, and

joke: 'Have you got any potatoes?' 'No, it's meat we haven't got here. Try next door for potatoes ... they haven't got any there.'

Freedom does count for something, however. On the intellectual front, for example, there has been one great improvement. Gone are the days when people had to sneak, at some risk, into mysterious back rooms to obtain copies of the banned work of a dissident – the man who is now President Havel perhaps, or one of the other members of the underground civil rights movement, Charter 77. At the same time, by a nice irony, the unloved works of Lenin, Brezhnev and the former Party Leader Gustáv Husák that so long adorned bookshop windows have been pulped to help to provide much needed paper.

Beer, please . . . morning and evening

Fortunately, no national upheaval, however severe, has ever resulted in a shortage of beer. There are three basic kinds in Czechoslovakia: standard draught beer (*vycepní*), bottled beer (*lezák*) and the various special brews. These special brews, which include a dozen or so well-known national brands as well as numerous local varieties, range in style from the popular *desítka* (at 10° proof) to the more sophisticated *dvanáctka* produced by the Prague-Smichov brewery or the original Pilsener from Plzen in south-western Bohemia. Another fine brew is the 7° proof black beer, an exceptionally thick and tasty drink served in a few rare establishments. The Czechs are immensely proud of all these beers – which are, indeed, widely regarded as the best in the world –

salaries have been unable to keep pace. To make things worse, the withdrawal of many state subsidies has produced widespread unemployment. People in the arts have been particularly badly hit, but even doctors and surgeons have found themselves hard pressed.

Food queues are also no longer a depressing feature of everyday life but prices have risen, so people look for bargains. The overlapping of the old socialist methods of distribution with new, free-market enterprises (chiefly aimed at making a quick profit) has led to enormous confusion. Czechoslovakia need not be a poor country – indeed, before the Second World War its standard of living was comparable with that of Britain or France – but that does not prevent fresh fruit, for example, from being virtually unobtainable, whatever the season. If you can afford to buy a decent piece of meat, it is something to celebrate; you invite your friends round to join in the festivities. More often, the meat ration is so gristly that it is suitable only for a goulash at best. The situation has improved over the last year or so as the problems of distribution are slowly ironed out. But a reminder of the bad old days is the wry

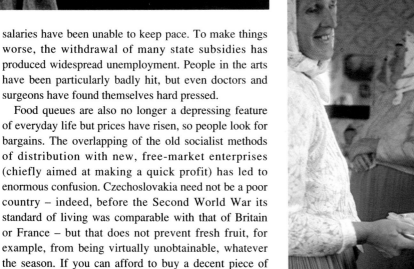

Marriages are still celebrated in traditional style in rural Slovakia. Everyone in the village is invited, as well as even the most distant relatives from outside it. The women wear neatly folded head-scarves, and everyone enjoys the numerous cakes that go with the occasion.

A snowfall muffles Prague's beautiful Charles Bridge, built in 1348 in the reign of the Emperor Charles IV and one of the oldest in Europe. On either side of the bridge rise statues of saints added in the 17th and 18th centuries, supposedly for the edification of passers-by. At its far end a fortified gateway leads into the old aristocratic quarters of Malá Strana and Hradcany. The domes of the former royal castle – now the home of the president – stand out beyond.

Czechoslovak flags hang from the patrician façades of Maly Rynecek (Small Square) at the heart of old Prague. On the left is one of the best of the capital's antikvariats which, with their second-hand books and old prints, have always been among the favourite retreats of Prague intellectuals.

knedlíky. The *knedlíky* are one of the great Czech specialities, a kind of dumpling made with flour and egg yolks and moulded into small cakes about as thick as a finger. They are extremely filling, and extremely popular; for special occasions they are sometimes made with potato flour. Another possible component of the midday meal is soup: a broth with meatballs floating in it perhaps, or a delicious *drstková*, whose key ingredient is tripe. The Czechs make some fine soups as well as beers, but the favourite, a rich peasant dish with potatoes and mushrooms, never appears in restaurants. Like the best *knedlíky*, it is only ever made at home.

Few people cook in the evenings. Around six o'clock, families will have a simple cold meal – unless, that is, somebody has thought to make some sweet *knedlíky*. These are eaten with fruit or jam, with melted butter or soured cream poured on top ... a meal in itself. After that, one of the younger members of the family may be

Customers tuck into an open-air meal in Prague's Mala Strana district. Eating and drinking establishments are divided into two main categories: pivnice *where you drink beer and* vinárna *where you drink wine.*

and most people's day is punctuated with regular trips for a quick drink.

The working day begins early – at seven, six, even five o'clock. Breakfast consists of ham and cheese on slices of rye bread, washed down with a cup of coffee (usually powdered coffee which never seems to dissolve properly). Then it is time for the day's first queue – at the bus or tram stop. Around mid-morning, after a few hours' work, comes a trip to the Automat (a sort of snack bar) and the first beer of the day, drunk standing at the bar from a tankard, with a few *chlebícky* – open sandwiches of hard-boiled egg, ham and fish roe. At midday it is time for lunch at the local *hospoda* (roughly equivalent to a French bistro). This involves another queue and then, in due course, more beers and one of a few standard dishes: pork (or perhaps goose, in winter) or a beef goulash spiced with paprika, all served with sent with a large jug to the nearest *vycep* (beer shop) to bring home a pint or two of draught beer. This is better than the bottled stuff, and a lot cheaper.

Prague nights

How to spend an evening out? This was more of a problem in the days of the Communists, who definitely preferred people to go to bed early. Nowadays, with the cinemas showing Western films and the theatres putting on long-censored plays, the choice is rather wider. None the less, memories of past events (not all of them bad) die hard. One attractive ritual at the end of an enjoyable evening in Prague is to pause a while in Wenceslas (Vaclav) Square – dominated by an equestrian statue of the 10th-century saint-ruler, who is also remembered in the English carol. Here, revellers buy a final round of beers and some barbecued sausages dipped in mustard, and look up at the balconies where, in the heady days of November 1989, Vaclav Havel and later Alexander Dubcek came out to announce the death throes of the old order.

Yet for all the attractions of theatres, cinemas and night clubs, many people still prefer the more traditional pleasures of the *pivnice* or *vinárna*. The *pivnice* is where you drink *pivo*, beer, and nothing else. In the country or poorer areas of the towns, it may be no more than a large room with a few tables covered with white cloths. Or there may be one long table with benches down each side, where customers knock back their drinks elbow to elbow. A few *pivnice* in Prague and Bratislava open onto courtyards or gardens, though open-air terraces in the style of France or Italy are rare. But the most typical and popular *pivnice* – many

claiming to have been doing business since the Middle Ages – are in huge, vaulted cellars. Some of these, such as Prague's famous U Fleku, also serve their own special brews.

The scene in a *pivnice* is animated in the extreme. You find your seats – it is best to get there by seven o'clock at the latest to be sure of a place – and call the waiter: '*Pane vrchní*!' He ploughs his way through the crowd towards you, a tray of frothing tankards in one hand. Deftly extracting pencil and pad from his breast pocket, he makes a note of your order: *malé pivo* (small beer), perhaps, if you are feeling cautious, or full-sized *dospely* (literally, 'adult beer') if you are bolder. The drinks flow and everybody becomes steadily more jovial. After a while, the whole room may burst into song. This is different from the Teutonic vigour of German beer singing. With the Czechs and Slovaks the melodies are more lingering, and there is always an elegant hint of melancholy. Finally, it is time to go home. The waiter comes, counts the pencil strokes on his pad and calculates the bill. As you pay and leave, he thanks you 'respectfully' for your custom – Czechoslovakia preserves much of the scrupulous politeness of the old Austro-Hungarian Empire.

The other favourite evening haunt of the Czechs and Slovaks, the *vinárna*, is where you drink *víno*, wine. Here the atmosphere is different and the clientele are mostly academics and intellectuals, young couples or the old or newer bourgeoisie, depending on the establishment. A *vinárna* is also generally smaller than a *pivnice*, with intimate corner tables and subdued lights, and is more elegant and expensive. But it is a good idea to arrive before seven or eight, even on weekday evenings. In Prague, the smartest *vinárnen* are in the baroque Mala Strana quarter or in the Old Town,

The writer Jaroslav Hasek (1883-1923) could claim some fame in a number of spheres – as a formidable drinker, a would-be politician, even as a dog barber. But he is chiefly remembered for his fictional creation, the Good Soldier Svejk. The innocent-seeming Svejk, wily hero of a novel set in the First World War, manages to extricate himself from the most impossible situations.

From May to September, the Václavské Námesti, Prague's main shopping street, is lined with numerous stalls where old ladies sell flowers from their gardens or from small suburban cooperatives.

The venerable Café Slavia is a favourite haunt of Prague's intellectuals. Propaganda posters celebrating the years of 'friendship' between the Czechoslovak and Soviet peoples have now all gone from the windows.

The paint may have faded from the buildings round Telc market square in southern Moravia, but they are still among Czechoslovakia's finest examples of mid-16th-century town architecture. Their restrained yet splendid ornamentation gives an idea of the wealth and sophistication of the region in centuries past.

Though baroque style is best known in grand 17th-century churches and palaces, in Bohemia it was widely adopted even for relatively modest buildings, and was still popular in the second half of the 19th century. This farm in Drahonice in southern Bohemia is typical of popular baroque. The farmhouse is on the left, a curved gable hiding the tiled roof.

Winter solaces

Winter, especially the months after Christmas and the New Year, is the season of balls, which are attended by people of all ages and backgrounds. Smartness is a keynote of these highly popular occasions; women dress up in all their finery, and though few men wear dinner jackets nowadays, there is usually a healthy sprinkling of black bow ties. Revellers exhausted by dancing can retire for a few minutes to enjoy brimming tankards of locally brewed beer in a refreshments room adjoining the ballroom.

Nostalgia is generally a strong element at such events. Many people go less for the dancing than for an opportunity to spend a pleasant evening with friends in surroundings where the faded, frequently art nouveau, elegance conjures up past glories. One popular place for balls is the Obecní Dum in central Prague, its chief attraction being a dozen large rooms decorated by the

In the ancient town of Cheb in western Bohemia, an 18th-century rococo front disguises the Gothic interior. Cheb was founded in the 10th century and its buildings preserve a splendid jumble of styles – Gothic, Renaissance, baroque and rococo.

and are not always easy to find. To reach the venerable Barberina, for example, you have to grope your way down the ill-lit corridors of an ancient building. Then you suddenly emerge into a room that encapsulates everyone's inner picture of an old-time central European interior: velvet-covered chairs, ceilings embossed with gold, long mirrors on the walls and statues of Greek gods and goddesses. At the far end of the room, a duo on piano and violin play airs with a vague Gypsy ring for the entertainment of the 20 or so privileged customers whom the dinner-jacketed maître d'hôtel has allowed in. Needless to say, there are no blue jeans or even corduroys in this sacred spot – they would be considered an unpardonable affront to the spirit of the place.

turn-of-the-century painter Alfons Mucha. White-jacketed waiters wheel trolleys laden with bottles of rare wines; people drink, dance and chat; the years seem to roll back. For one evening at least the everyday problems of modern life can be forgotten – the queues, the food shortages, the difficulties of earning enough money. *Za Rakouska* ... ('In Austrian times ...') is a phrase that often surfaces on such occasions. Through

from the patisserie. The Czechs, like the Viennese (whose *Sachertorte* made with chocolate and apricot jam is as much loved in Prague as in Austria), have a definite weakness for cakes and sweet things – *Bez práce nejsou koláce* is a typical local proverb: 'No work, no cakes'. Czech specialities include *buchta* (a kind of doughnut) and *prazsky kolác* or 'Prague cake' – a pastry cake filled with vanilla-flavoured cream. Apple

In Communist days, despite the collectivisation of agriculture, peasants were still allowed their own small allotments where they managed to grow miraculous amounts of fruit and vegetables. As the laborious process of de-collectivisation' gets under way, these allotments are still the main-stay of local food production.

the rosy lenses of hindsight, those times seem to have been sweeter.

The other great treat of winter is the snows, which arrive late in Czechoslovakia, usually closer to Easter than Christmas. This time it is the children who celebrate. Each weekend crowds of them converge on Prague's main parks, tugging their toboggans behind them. The slopes of the Grobavka Park, in particular, are a favourite tobogganing spot.

Returning home, their cheeks burning from the cold and excitement, the children can look forward to yet another treat: hot chocolate and *bábovka* (cakes and pastries), either home-made by their mothers or bought

strudel is another favourite, here as in southern Germany and Austria.

The place to enjoy the full array of these cakes is the *kavarna*, the huge, plushly furnished café, also reminiscent of Vienna. The juke box, piped music and other American-style 'barbarities' which long preceded the arrival of democracy in Czechoslovakia have yet to make any impression on these hushed and dusty sanctuaries. In the afternoons, old ladies arrive for coffee – either Viennese (with whipped cream floating on top) or Turkish – and cakes chosen from the counter. Old gentlemen while away the hours in front of newspapers perched on special wickerwork frames with handles for turning the pages. Nobody would dream of asking for a proletarian beer in such a spot ... any more than they would ask for tea in a *pivnice*. The *kavárna* and *pivnice* represent two poles in a world where, despite 40 years of socialism, the old class barriers are still alive in many people's minds.

On the other hand, the *kavárnen* are not exclusively the domain of the elderly and respectable. Many have long traditions as meeting places for artists and intellectuals. The Café Slavia, for example, opposite Prague's National Theatre, was a favourite drinking place in the early years of this century of the poet Rainer Maria Rilke. And Kafka was a regular at the Café Arco in the Old Town. For them it would have been numerous *dve deci* (literally, 'two decilitres') of white wine that fuelled their discussions.

Dollar power

As in the other countries of the former Eastern Bloc, one highly characteristic institution survived until recently: the state-owned hard-currency shop or Tuzex, where you could buy just about anything – provided you paid in foreign currency, chiefly dollars, marks and pounds ... The new authorities are no better placed than were their Communist predecessors to buy non-essential imports with hard currency and then sell them locally for Czech crowns. As a result, Western consumer goods, whether instant coffee, Swiss chocolate, clothes, foreign drinks or cars, are available only at exorbitant prices. A bottle of whisky, for example, at 400 crowns is five or six times the average daily wage.

This explains the importance of the Tuzex. You could exchange a few dollars or marks for 'Tuzex vouchers' at a bank (they rarely bothered to ask awkward questions about the provenance of the currency) and all kinds of luxuries could be yours. It explains too, the supposedly clandestine traffic in foreign currency (which everybody knew about and most people practised when they had the opportunity), not to mention the whispered '*Geld wechseln* ... Change money' in the ear of Western-looking tourists or 'Tuzex foreigners', as opposed to the less-favoured visitors from Bulgaria or other East

Mushrooms, either fresh or dried, have a prominent place in Czechoslovak cooking. Among the best-loved of all the various peasant soups is one made with mushrooms and potatoes.

Two peasant women from the High Tatra Mountains survey the display in a flower shop at Levoca in Slovakia. No man-made show, however, is likely to match the natural splendour of their native highlands.

European countries. How else were local people to obtain the benefits of hard currency? For, unlike their neighbours in Poland, they receive comparatively little assistance from émigré relatives.

There is another reason for this flourishing black market. The Czechs, who are naturally curious about foreign cultures and traditions and often speak at least one foreign language, like to travel. But the foreign currency allowances are extremely low, so once again they have to resort to the unofficial market to buy the marks, francs or pounds they need for a short, cheap holiday in the West. In the old days, hopeful travellers had to wait patiently to be granted a passport; nowadays they have to wait for currency. Alternatively, those in certain academic or industrial jobs may be lucky enough to get an invitation from a Western university or company; but these too, though fairly lavishly dispensed in the first flush of excitement after 1989, have recently begun to dry up. So have any hopes of working in the West. Since Czechoslovakia is now a democracy, its people no longer have any right to political refugee status, and Western European governments, terrified of an immigrant influx from the East, are putting up increasingly stiff barriers against would-be workers.

Rebuilding the ruined house

In Vaclav Havel, the Czechs and Slovaks are lucky enough to have an inspiring figurehead to preside over the difficult transition from dictatorship to democracy.

This ingeniously designed mug, from which a woman is sipping at Karlovy Vary (Carlsbad), has a built-in straw. The town is famous for its spa waters, its porcelain and crystalware, and its annual film festival.

The former dissident, imprisoned several times by the Communists, has undoubtedly spared his countrymen many of the false starts and disillusionments that could have accompanied, and perhaps ultimately derailed, the process of rebuilding their country. With the quiet backing of other former dissidents and former Communists such as Dubcek (who returned from internal exile in 1989 to become Speaker of the Czechoslovak Parliament), he has sought to avoid the more brutal aspects of the return to a market economy, yet without glossing over the immense difficulties involved in the enterprise.

The economy inherited by his government, for all its strength relative to those of most other Eastern European countries, is beset with numerous problems. Industry is antiquated and incapable of surviving without huge state subsidies. Moreover, it is responsible for appalling pollution – which is endangering not only the country's forests and rivers (particularly in Slovakia), but also the health of those working in industry. 'What originally seemed to be a neglected house is, in fact, a ruin,' was President Havel's bleak warning in a New Year address at the start of 1991, after just over a year in office.

The departure of the Communists has unearthed more than just economic problems. In common with many of its neighbours, Czechoslovakia has, for example, a problem of nationalities, chiefly the traditional rivalry between Czechs and Slovaks. Although both are Slavic peoples with languages so similar that a Slovak can understand a Czech without difficulty, the two peoples have never properly blended – in the days of the Austro-Hungarian Empire of the Habsburgs, the Czechs had closer ties with the Austrians, the Slovaks (rather unwillingly) with the Hungarians.

Many Slovaks feel that the Czechs (who outnumber

Western Bohemia's spa waters have been known for their healing properties since the Middle Ages, but came into their own in the 19th century. Kings and emperors, great aristocrats, famous writers, composers and artists, all gathered at fashionable resorts such as Marienbad (now Mariánské Lázne) and Carlsbad (Karlovy Vary). Nowadays the spas play host to more modest patients, but the imposing neo-baroque buildings remain.

Medieval gravestones in the cemetery of Prague's former Jewish ghetto witness the important part long played by the Jewish community in the life of the capital. Some of Prague's most famous sons, such as the writer Franz Kafka, were Jewish.

them roughly two to one) discriminate against them, and there is a growing nationalist movement within the Slovak part of the federal republic; some Slovak leaders are even demanding outright independence. On top of that, Czechoslovakia has other minorities each with their own grievances: the ethnic Hungarians of southern Slovakia; a substantial Gypsy community (some 750,000 strong), again in Slovakia; and large numbers of Vietnamese immigrant workers who arrived in industrial cities throughout the country during the 1970s. All these peoples help to enhance the diversity of the Czechoslovak nation; all equally, with their various separatist ambitions, add more problems to the impressive heap facing the country.

Daunting though the difficulties are, there is definitely a new spirit in Czechoslovakia. Within a year of the 1989 revolution, Prague in particular seemed a new city. Most of the visible trappings of state socialism – the innumerable statues of Lenin and Stalin, for example – had been stripped away, and there was a new excitement in the air.

Nowhere was the transformation more noticeable than in the former royal castle of Hradcany, since 1918 the seat of presidential power, which dominates much of the city from its hill on the west bank of the Vltava river. Gone were the tired bureaucrats of the old order;

Slovakia preserves more of the old ways of life than many other parts of Eastern Europe. At weddings, sumptuously embroidered traditional costumes are still often worn by the bride and groom and many of the chief attendants.

Traditional costumes have more or less disappeared from Bohemia, except in the Chod region around Domazlice in the west. In the villages here, old women and young girls still favour red or black headscarves, white blouses and flounced skirts with red and orange stripes.

in their place the castle's corridors and offices had been taken over by a younger generation of democrats, many of them ex-dissidents. One symbolic change was the return of some of the old aristocracy. In the summer of 1990, Prince Charles von Schwarzenberg, born in 1937, a minor member of a famous local family, returned to the Hradcany as one of Havel's most trusted advisors. By some administrative error on the part of the Communist authorities, the millionaire businessman-prince, who had spent most of his adult life in Austria, had never lost his Czechoslovak nationality.

The stresses of freedom

Under the Communists, the position of Czecho-slovakia's writers, academics and intellectuals was even more precarious than that of their fellows in the other Eastern Block countries, apart from Romania. After the crushing of the 1968 Prague Spring in particular, the authorities became more and more heavy-handed in their response to dissent. Increasing numbers of the intelligentsia were imprisoned or suddenly stripped of their posts (often under the flimsiest of pretexts) and then forced into an extraordinary assortment of menial jobs in order to survive.

One legacy of this era of repression has been entirely positive: an almost unassailable solidarity and mutual respect among the intelligentsia. This has survived the

Old and new rub shoulders at Nové Mesto nad Váhom in Slovakia. These peasant women in traditional dress have come down from their villages high in the Carpathian Mountains, but do not look out of place in Nové Mesto's modern streets.

The wandering puppet master was for centuries as familiar a sight on the highways and byways of Bohemia as the tinker. Only with the upheavals of this century have puppet theatres begun to lose their appeal for the country people.

return of freedom and lent the country's cultural life a special vibrancy. Since 1989, motley bands of university-educated ex-prisoners, night watchmen, window cleaners, charwomen, hotel porters, factory workers, street musicians, waiters and farm labourers have made their way back from ten to fifteen years of internal exile and imprisonment to take up once more their positions in the theatres, hospitals, universities, broadcasting studios, newspaper offices and publishing houses. In the process they have kindled a striking cultural revolution. A thing of the past is the evening seminar when friends met secretly in somebody's flat to discuss protest action or simply the new ideas filtering in from the West. So is the constant fear of a knock on the door heralding a police swoop and the disappearance of one or more members of the group for several months or years. Instead, former *samizdat* (clandestine) journals are now openly published and flourishing; the theatres and cabarets are full and free; and no one need fear to express openly their true thoughts.

As so often in such situations, the new liberty has engendered its own problems. In this respect, exiles returning from abroad are in perhaps the most difficult position. Because they have to find their feet in a country they left several years previously, they cannot share in the significant experiences of the time in the same way as their fellows who suffered internal exile or imprisonment. The return home, so long looked forward to, often proves traumatic and disillusioning. Whether consciously or not, those who stayed behind frequently make their returning colleagues feel inadequate, even unwanted. As well as adapting to a society that has changed radically since they last knew it, returning exiles have to contend with an underlying hostility.

In some ways, this gap in understanding is similar to the barrier between the people who experienced the tragedy of 1968 and their children and grandchildren who came after it. On the eve of the victorious demonstrations in the winter of 1989, it was the parents who urged caution, scarcely able to believe that what had failed in 1968 could succeed now. Their offspring, by contrast, were determined to make their presence felt on the streets, confident that the time for change really had arrived. In the event, they were proved right. It was they who made the 'velvet revolution'. But the same people now have to pursue the second revolution that, almost alone in post-1989 Eastern Europe, Havel and many Czechs and Slovaks still aspire to – the revolution that reconciles the strengths of the market economy with the persistent dreams of a truly egalitarian society. Not only that: they will also have to make a workable entity of the Czech and Slovak Federal Republic (to give it its official name), with its often conflicting nationalist aspirations and traditions.

Winter in Central Europe is the time for public balls and dances in the towns and for skiing and tobogganing in the mountains. Snow shrouding the village church and the pine woods rising behind is another familiar winter scene; and young and old alike are wrapped up against the cold.

Hungary

Set in the heart of the Danube basin, Hungary is Central Europe *par excellence*. The country is surprisingly small – only 325 miles from west to east. Yet it has an impact disproportionate to its size. Its people, the Magyars, are neither Slav nor German and are fiercely proud of their identity. They are a spirited nation – outstanding in science, music and literature – who strained for years at the leash of Communism. They were already experimenting with free-market economics before the world had heard of *perestroika*, and were among the first to take advantage of the new democratic liberty that swept Eastern Europe in 1989.

*Sunset on Lake Balaton.
With its miles of beaches
offering safe bathing and its
plentiful resorts, Balaton is
land-locked Hungary's
favourite holiday area.
In winter it doubles as a
gigantic skating-rink.*

*Mending nets at a fisherman's
hut near Lake Kondor in the
Kiskúnság National Park. The
park covers more than 100
square miles, and consists of
protected marshland, steppes
and pastures. Among the many
species of fish found in
Hungary are carp, pike, roach,
sturgeon and sheath-fish.*

Previous page: *One of the
celebrated flower painters of
Kalocsa. Floral motifs are
used in embroidery, and to
decorate furniture and houses.
The paints, in six colours, are
mixed with milk.*

Hungarian Rhapsodies

The river Danube divides Hungary into two large and very different regions: the Great Hungarian Plain (or Nagy Magyar Alföld) to the east, and Transdanubia (Dunántúl) to the west. The Great Hungarian Plain is in turn cut in two by a river of its own, the Tisza, which rises in the Carpathian Mountains, flows southwards across Hungary, and joins the Danube a few miles north of Belgrade. It is known as the 'yellow Tisza' because of the immense quantities of sand it transports. Both the Danube and the Tisza were prone to massive flooding in the past, but have now been tamed, through flow-regulation and the construction of many hundreds of miles of levées.

At the heart of the Great Plain is the Puszta – 'the bare land' – a region of vast open spaces, dazzling light and long hot summers. Bareback-riding *csikós* (guardians) patrol the stud farms, and long-horned sheep and sturdy grey Hungarian cattle – an old resilient stock much used for cross-breeding – graze under an immense sky. There were once some forests here, but these were cut down in the 16th and 17th centuries during the Turkish occupation. With the trees gone, the land became semi-desert prairie. Yet now, through irrigation, the draining of marshes and re-planting, the Great Plain has revived.

Its desolate beauty remains, however, and the rich wildlife of the region is protected in several National Parks. If the catalogue of Hungarian fauna no longer includes bears, wolves and beavers, as it once did, there are still wild boar, foxes, hares, duck, pheasant and deer in abundance, providing sport for the hunter and meat for the peasant's table.

A lake as big as a sea

Transdanubia is a greener and gentler land, with a mild climate and rolling hills. At its centre lies Lake Balaton, 48 miles long by a maximum of 9 wide, with a surface area of some 230 square miles. It is a freshwater inland 'sea' complete with beaches, holiday resorts, fishing boats, ferries, shipyards and harbours. Legend has it that the lake appeared when a drunken goatherd struck a rock and released a spring whose waters drowned him and his scattered flock. On stormy days, so the legend goes, you can still see the white goats gambolling among the waves ...

Geologists date the formation of the lake's bed to the late Pleistocene Epoch (around one million years ago), although it is believed to have been flooded only 20,000 years ago, following volcanic eruptions. The River Zala and several streams now keep the lake supplied with its 2.4 billion cubic yards of water, shared by forty-two species of fish – including carp, bream, eel, catfish, perch, pike and sturgeon.

Balaton is highly popular with holidaymakers and weekenders, and both the lake itself and the roads leading to it are crowded during the summer. The lake's alkaline waters are said to have healing properties, and its warm summer temperatures (up to 25°C, or 77°F) make for exceptionally pleasant bathing. In winter the surface freezes solid and provides a vast arena for skating and other winter-sports – such as *fakutya*, which involves propelling oneself in a sled across the ice with the aid of a pair of sticks.

Among the many attractions on the northern shore are the Tihany Peninsula, now a nature reserve, and the health resort of Balatonfüred, where in the second quarter of the 19th century leading artists, intellectuals and politicians used to gather informally each summer, giving new impetus to a revival of Hungarian national culture. Farther west and a little inland is the ancient spa of Hévíz, with its warm-water lake ringed with lilies and fed by vigorous hot springs. At the south-west tip of

Game is plentiful in Hungary, and the close season is strictly observed, making the country a paradise for hunters.

Lake Balaton is the splendid Festetics Mansion at Keszthely, built in the 18th century by a family of enlightened and reforming landowners. One of them, Count György Festetics, founded an agricultural college here in 1797 – the oldest such institution in Europe.

The southern shore, whose gently sloping sand beaches and shallow waters are safe for children, is largely devoted to bathing resorts. A canal starts at the town of Siófok, connecting the lake to the Danube via a series of river navigations.

Hungary is particularly rich in thermal springs – only Iceland has more. The water in the springs is heated through contact with hot or molten volcanic rock beneath the earth and, apart from providing hot water for bathing, has long been considered health-giving. In the 1st century AD the Romans found the hot springs at Aquincum, as had the Celts before them, and turned the town into a provincial capital: its extensive ruins can still be seen today in a suburb of Budapest. During their 150-year stay, the Turks built numerous baths, many of which are still working. Budapest has some 31 thermal baths, fed by 120 hot springs, and there are famous spas at Hajdúszoboszló, Balf, Balatonfüred, Bükkfürdö, Gyula, Harkány, Hévíz, Parád and Zalakaros, as well as dozens of lesser-known ones. Exploratory drilling for oil often reveals more. The waters are used to fill heated swimming pools and provide central heating for greenhouses. They continue to have medical applications too, in the treatment of rheumatism and diseases of the heart, circulation and skin.

To the north of Lake Balaton rise the Bakony mountains, whose forests were once the domain of the *betyárs*, a likeable set of brigands – Hungarian Robin Hoods – who set the countryside to rights with their own brand of rough justice. As a souvenir of the good old days, a local travel agency organises specially-staged 'hold-ups' by the *betyárs* on tourist coaches. These provide all the thrills of a Wild West stage-coach robbery with none of the dangers. Afterwards, to show that there are no hard feelings, tourists and *betyárs* get together to knock back a few drinks at one of the local highwaymen's inns.

This delightful, bucolic region has been spared the agonies of much of Hungarian history. Traditions are strong, as a visit to the historic towns of Veszprém, Sopron, or Pécs will prove. Yet even here, despite the well-preserved buildings, time has not stood still. At Sopron, close to the Austrian border, they have the first-ever East European branch of Marks and Spencer.

Transdanubia is the most economically active part of the country. This is largely thanks to a wealth of natural resources: coal at Komló and Tatabánya, bauxite at Ajka and Almásfüzítö, uranium at Pécs. There are steel works at Györ and Dunaújváros, electrical and automotive industries at Székesfehérvár, and food packaging and production at Bábolna.

The East

North-eastern Hungary is mountainous, consisting of the Mátra, Bükk and Zemplén ranges. The word 'mountains' (*hegy* in Hungarian) is somewhat deceptive. The highest of them, Mount Kékes, is 3330

The village of Hollókö in northern Hungary, where the old buildings and customs are lovingly preserved by inhabitants who wear traditional costume and speak an old dialect of Hungarian.

The Magyars are early risers. The market opens at 6am and reaches a peak of activity between 9 and 11. This old peasant woman will not go home, though, until all her radishes are sold.

On a cold and frosty morning, a shooting party sets out in search of game. They may come back with deer, hare, partridges or pheasants, which are all in plentiful supply.

Paprika was introduced by Christopher Columbus from America to Western Europe, and by the Turks from Persia to central Europe. The small yellow, green or red fruits are highly aromatic. They have been an essential ingredient of Hungarian cookery since the early 19th century.

After harvesting, the red peppers are hung up to dry in the sun, then taken for milling into paprika powder. This is packaged and sold according to its quality: extra sweet, sweet, 'rose' (mildly sharp), and sharp.

Many geese are kept in Hungary for the production of foie gras – fine goose-liver pâté, one of the country's most successful exports.

feet (compare Mount Snowdon at 3560 feet). These are not the Himalayas, or even the Alps. Lovers of the mountains of Britain will feel at home here, for this is ideal walking country, with the most dramatic scenery in Hungary. The Szalajka valley, accessible only on foot or by narrow gauge railway, is particularly beautiful, as is Szilvásvárad with its trout lakes and stud farms, where the famous Lipizzaner horses are bred for use at the Spanish Riding School in Vienna.

The Lipizzaner, named after the Austrian stud farm at Lipizza near Trieste where they were first bred in 1580, come from a mixed ancestry of Andalusian, Arabian and local Karst horses. They are quite small (around 15 hands at most), usually white or grey, with a long back and powerful build. Their good nature and intelligence have made them particularly suitable for the 18th-century *haute école* disciplines of dressage as practised at the Spanish Riding School. The joy here, though, is to see them running wild in the meadows.

In this same region are the vast limestone caves at Aggtelek, with the rock formations suggesting fairy castles and haunted caverns; one 14-mile cave crosses the Czechoslovakian frontier underground. At the Jósvafö caves, the biggest stalagmites in the world can be found, weighing – it is said – over a thousand tons. Historic towns in the area include Miskolc, Szerencs, Sárospatak, and the village of Tokaj, renowned for its wine – which no less a figure than Louis XIV called 'the wine of kings, and king of wines'.

Tokay is a sweet wine, made from furmint grapes which are left on the vines, like those of Sauternes, to grow overripe and develop 'noble rot', which greatly increases their sugar content. The resulting sweet must is mixed with that of ordinary ripe grapes to produce Tokay. According to wine expert Hugh Johnson, a good bottle will have a 'silky texture, a haunting fragrance and flavour of mingled fruit and butter and caramel and the breath of the Bodrog [river] among October vines'.

Despite a dwindling rural population, peasant traditions remain strong in Hungary, and since the demise of the Communist regime, everyone's dream of owning a piece of land looks like coming true.

A replica of a traditional peasant home at the folk museum, Szenna (far right). The table stood opposite the oven in the large communal room. After meals this would be cleared, leaving only the bread in the place of honour. The bed is piled high with the family's eiderdowns and pillows. The painted chests store linen and clothes.

The main elements of Hungarian peasant costume are skirt, blouse, waistcoat, apron, headscarf, stockings and boots or slippers. Waistcoats, aprons and scarves are usually brightly and beautifully embroidered.

Miska wine jugs are made of glazed and painted pottery, and are often inscribed with the date of manufacture and the name of the person for whom they were made.

As if that were not enough, a special version, which is now virtually unobtainable, was made from the fermented oozings of only the sweetest grapes, and exclusively reserved for the use of monarchs on their deathbeds. One imagines them dying with angelic smiles on their lips.

The first Hungarians

According to the so-called 'legend of the white horse', the Magyars, under their leader Arpád, sent a messenger to Sviatopluk, king of Moravia, when they arrived at the frontiers of what is today their land. The messenger brought gifts: a white horse with a saddle and bridle of gold. Sviatopluk was a somewhat innocent character, who accepted these gifts and offered in exchange the earth and water of his country. Arpád and his men took him at his word and moved in.

Charming as this story is, one would have to be as naive as Sviatopluk to swallow it. The fact is that Hungary was taken by force of arms in the late 9th century. The conquest, known as *honfoglalás* by Hungarian historians, was made easier by the fact that the country was a sort of no man's land between the Germans and the Slavs, left half-empty after the departure of the Romans at the end of the 4th century AD and the subjection of the Avars by Charlemagne in AD 795.

The ancestors of the Finno-Ugrian peoples and the Magyars are believed to have lived around the upper reaches of the Volga and Kama rivers in western

Siberia. Around 2000 BC some of them moved westwards to the Baltic, settling in the lands that were eventually to become Finland and Estonia. The rest moved south to the steppes north of the Caspian Sea, where they lived as nomadic herdsmen. In the early 9th century they moved westwards to the river Don, and later that century west again to the area of present-day Hungary. By this time they had clearly developed formidable fighting skills, lording it over the resident Slavs and Huns and running raids northwards to Bremen, south to Otranto and Constantinople, and west as far as the Pyrenees.

At this time they were organised into seven tribes or hordes, each with a hereditary chieftain placed at the head of a number of different clans. Clan members were free, but kept slaves collected in their frequent raids. However their mobile, warlike way of life was soon to come to an end. In 955 they were badly defeated by the German emperor Otto I at Augsburg, and they decided to hang up their swords. They made peace with their neighbours and converted to Christianity. King Stephen I (who reigned from AD 1000 to 1038) dismantled the tribal structure and replaced it with a feudal system, similar to those existing throughout the rest of Europe. Of their earlier culture they retained little but the language – part of the Finno-Ugric linguistic group – related only to Finnish and Estonian among European languages.

Houses built of mud and straw

The early architecture of Hungary was determined by three influences: the semi-nomadic economy, the materials available, and, when they came to build churches and palaces, by Byzantine and European models. The best of this architecture was destroyed in the Tatar invasion of the mid-13th century, and then again by the Turkish occupation in the 16th and 17th centuries. After each invasion, efforts at reconstruction were made, but until the 18th century no style or tendency had time to develop fully, and no continuous heritage was established.

On the Great Hungarian Plain, traditional houses were made of mud or clay and wood. The mud was packed into shuttering (similar to that used in the making of modern reinforced concrete) to make walls. Roofs were thatched with reeds or straw over a wooden frame. There was a hearth without a chimney, the smoke escaping through gaps in the roof and eaves.

With the development of agriculture came villages and *tanyák*, or farmsteads built among the fields. The *tanyák* began as summer working homes, but gradually became permanent farms. Until quite recently, the Great Plain was dotted with these whitewashed *tanyák*, scattered around large primitive villages.

The country people now form a dwindling sector of the population (currently 20 per cent of a total of 10.5 million), but their way of life and thought, and their extraordinary faces, have been preserved for posterity in the films of Miklós Jancsó, István Gaál, Ferenc Kósa and Zoltán Huszárik. The traditional farms too are disappearing, saved only by city-dwellers buying them

Long-horned Hungarian sheep
(raczka) *at Bugac in the
Kiskunság National Park.
The herdsman* (juhász) *wears
the traditional waistcoat,
hat and wide-sleeved shirt,
and rides a donkey.*

The nimble and shaggy-coated
puli *or Hungarian sheepdog is
black, white or grey and no
more than 18 inches tall. It is
regarded as one of the world's
most intelligent breeds.*

up as holiday homes. (You will often see '*Tanyát
keresek*' – 'Farmhouse wanted' – in the small ads
section of Hungarian newspapers.)

Mud houses are a good deal less fragile than one
might think, and many of them have managed to last for
several centuries. Churches and ramparts were built on
the same principle. Some of the finest specimens of
peasant architecture have been dismantled and
reconstructed at the two open-air museums of
Zalaegerszeg and Szentendre.

Builders and destroyers

A different type of village is found in Transdanubia,
where stone was available for building. The best
examples of medieval architecture, such as the churches
at Ják, Lébény and Pannonhalma, are somewhat off the
main tourist routes, in the Zala and Vas regions. Much,
however, was destroyed over the centuries by invaders,
and the full beauty and opulence of medieval art in
Hungary can now only be imagined with the help of
archaeology and written records.

The same is true of Renaissance art, which
flourished under the patronage of the brilliant and
splendour-loving King Matthias Corvinus (1458-90), its
development rudely cut short by the Turkish capture of
Buda in 1541 and the subsequent century and a half of
Ottoman occupation. When the Turks were expelled in
the 1680s, Hungary came under Habsburg rule,
adopting the prevalent baroque style of architecture,
which was influenced at first largely by the Italians, and
later by the Austrians, Germans and French.

Subjection to the Habsburgs was never welcomed by
the Hungarians. They made several attempts, both
military and political, to become independent, notably
in 1703 and 1848, when the Emperor Franz Joseph had
to ask the Russians for help in suppressing the rebellion.
Finally, weakened by defeats at the hands of the Italians
and the Prussians, Austria accepted a measure of

Hungarian independence under the Compromise of 1867, which turned the Habsburg empire into a Dual Monarchy (Austria-Hungary).

This arrangement lasted only until the end of the First World War, but it brought Hungary out of its backward colonial state with the development of agriculture, industry and commerce, railways, roads and town-planning.

Budapest became the capital in 1873, with the unification of the towns of Pest (on the left bank of the Danube), Buda (right bank) and Obuda (north of Buda). It was then that tramways and sewers were built, and boulevards laid out through the new residential and commercial quarters of Pest. Many of the buildings were in the Hungarian version of the art nouveau style of *belle époque* Paris. Cafés and cultural life flourished; and Budapest began to rival Vienna as the smartest city of Central Europe.

Even after two devastating wars, Budapest retains to this day much of its *fin de siècle* charm and fascination, with the Buda hills rolling scenically away from the Danube, and city and river together forming one of the most beautiful urban landscapes in the world.

Despite the embellishment of the capital and other chosen centres at the turn of the century, however, it has to be said that the general stagnation under the Austro-Hungarian monarchy, the poverty of building materials and frequent wars have left a grim heritage to the 20th century. A survey of housing in 1930 showed 98 per cent of dwellings consisting of one floor only, 75 per cent built of mud and clay, and only 50 per cent having drinking water.

In the dismantling of the Austro-Hungarian Empire that took place at the Paris Peace Conference at the end of the First World War, Hungary lost 70 per cent of its territory and 60 per cent of its population to the neighbouring countries of Yugoslavia, Romania, Czechoslovakia and Austria. This caused inevitable resentment, making Hungary a natural ally of Hitler's Germany in the 1930s – a relationship which was strengthened by a common determination to resist Communism. Apart from a brief Communist experiment

Woodmen at work in a forest in the north-east of the country. Charcoal was long used by industry and is now in demand again with the fashion for barbecuing.

under Béla Kun in 1919, Hungary between the wars was run by the conservative government of Miklós Horthy, a retired admiral of some military ability who made the fatal mistake of allying himself with Hitler. This alliance turned sour in 1944, and Hungary was overrun by the Germans, who were in turn expelled six months later by the Russians.

The devastation of the Second World War was followed by nearly half a century of Communism. This began in the Stalinist style with the setting up of a police state under the loathed Mátyás Rákosi. Following Stalin's death in 1953, and Khrushchev's denunciation of his policies in 1956, Rákosi was replaced and a reform movement began to grow. This culminated in the popular uprising of October 1956, which was savagely crushed by the Russian army – an event which shocked the world. For more than thirty years thereafter, Hungary was led by János Kádár, who managed to transform himself from a puppet of the Russians into one of the least dependent of Eastern European leaders, running a comparatively open regime.

In the post-war years a process of rapid urbanisation and industrialisation transformed the face of Hungary. It all happened very quickly. Towns doubled in size; the capital, swelling at an alarming rate, became home to a fifth of the country's population; and the old clay houses gave way to ugly modern tower blocks. Speed and economy were the bywords in the race to modernise the country and, at the same time, to house the rapidly growing urban workforce.

There have been efforts recently to bring beauty back to the cities. Traditional buildings and historic streets have been restored, notably in Budapest, Kecskemét and Sopron. But the monsters of the Stalinist years – industrial towns such as Dunaújváros and Komló – are reminders of a more brutal and utilitarian age.

A nation of poets and musicians

An agreeable way of discovering Hungary's history is to read her poets, many of whom have been translated into English. Each great moment of history has had its lyrical exponent: the Renaissance poet of love and military adventure, Bálint Balassi; Miklós Zrínyi, with his 17th-century epic of the defence of Szigetvár against the Turks; Sándor Petöfi, the 19th-century poet of independence and revolution, who was killed in battle against the Russians at the age of twenty-six; the Romantic patriot Mihály Vörösmarty; the modernist radical and controversialist Endre Ady (1877-1919); Attila József (1905-37), poet of the suffering working class; and Miklós Radnóti (1907-44), Hungary's most outspoken opponent of fascism, who was killed while a prisoner of the Germans in Yugoslavia.

'Hungarians,' it is said, 'think in poetry.' And poetry certainly holds a privileged place in the national culture,

A young horseman and his mount take a well-earned rest. The horse's unusual posture and the boy's grumpy expression suggest that they are quite blasé about being photographed by tourists.

A bareback riding stunt man from the Puszta shows off his skill in a show for tourists at Hortobágy.

A csikós *waters his horse at a trough. The traditional costume of these horsemen includes a dark blue shirt, wide pleated trousers and this curious black hat with a broad upturned brim.*

with frequent recitals in theatres and on the radio. Poetry sells well too. Even a newcomer's work will be given a print-run that only established poets get in Britain.

The Hungarians are a musically gifted nation too, with a rich folk tradition which was recorded and analysed by two of the greatest of this century's composers, Béla Bartók (1881-1945) and Zoltán Kodály (1882-1967). Kodály's educational methods are in use throughout the world, and have contributed to the exceptionally high level of musical literacy in Hungary. Franz (Ferenc in Hungarian) Liszt, the great 19th-century pianist and composer, was a Hungarian too, and Joseph Haydn spent thirty of the happiest and most productive years of his life as musical director at the magnificent Esterházy Palace – 'the Hungarian Versailles' – in Fertöd.

Colourful women's costumes in the village of Hollókö. They may wear up to fifteen petticoats under their skirts. Girls wear white or red necklaces, women green or blue, and old women no necklaces at all.

A round dance known as the karikázó. Once danced to an unaccompanied singing voice, it is divided into two parts: a long, slow introduction, and a short, lively conclusion.

Quality of life

Even under Communist rule, Hungary enjoyed a level of prosperity unusual in the Eastern Bloc. You could, for instance, find cars of all the leading European makes on the streets of Budapest. Books, rents, theatre and opera seats, were all reasonably priced. Such things give a certain tone to life.

The Hungarians are great eaters and drinkers too – their enthusiasm frequently overflowing the constraints of normal meal-times. Snack bars (*bisztró*, *büfé*), cafés (*eszpresszo*) and wine-bars (*borozó*) are everywhere, with locals constantly calling in for a little something to stave off a mid-morning or mid-afternoon craving.

Hungarian specialities include goulash (*gulyásleves*) and morello cherry soup (*meggyleves*), stews of fish, beef or pork, chicken paprika (*paprikáscsirke*), stuffed cabbage and peppers, and a dazzling range of desserts including strudels, pancakes, cakes and chocolate cream puddings. Wines are plentiful and various, as are many types of brandy and *pálinka* (eau-de-vie) such as *barack* made from apricots, or *cseresznye*, made from cherries. These are often served as an apéritif or even in the middle of the day. Apricot *pálinka* is particularly delicious, though one to be wary of, at least in the daytime. It gives off a beautiful flowery scent of fresh apricots when you uncork the bottle, but it has a massive kick when you actually drink it. Beer is usually lager, though a dark brew similar to brown ale can be found, and is frequently drunk with sausages, of which the Hungarians produce a bewildering and magnificent variety. With all this temptation around, it is not surprising perhaps that 30 per cent of the population is overweight, according to Ministry of Health statistics.

And yet the Hungarians like to keep fit. Sport plays a major part in their lives. There are good facilities in the major towns, and even the smallest village has its football pitch. There are numerous amateur sporting events around the country, and Hungary's Olympic athletes have an excellent record, winning a total of 123 gold medals, 110 silver, and 137 bronze in all Games up to 1988. Soccer remains the most popular sport, but water polo, fencing, boxing and handball also attract large crowds of spectators. Walking is a favourite pastime with both young and old, particularly in the form of organised expeditions.

The Hungarians, like the British, are inveterate gardeners. The pull of the earth is strong, with everyone dreaming of owning a *birtok*, a piece of land where they can grow flowers, fruit and vegetables, put up a simple hut, and get together with family and friends at weekends.

Gypsy violins

Thanks to Hollywood and the tourist industry, the music of the Hungarian Gypsies has become so well known as to become a cliché. Even if you have never sat in a restaurant at the start of a love affair with a dangerous

A young beauty from Kalocsa, where the traditional arts of floral painting and embroidery on lace continue to flourish.

and beautiful Communist spy, while a dark-skinned violinist whips up the romantic atmosphere among the flickering candles, the scene is somehow familiar ... Still, the combination of good wine, food and Gypsy music makes for a wonderful sense of conviviality, and it is here, gathered in restaurants ten or a dozen to a table, singing, eating and drinking, that the Hungarians really let themselves go.

The music itself tends to be a mixture of Gypsy tunes, popular songs, old favourites from opera and operetta, and *magyar nóta* – songs composed by musicians such as Dóczy, Serly, Simonffy or Pista Dankó – a Gypsy whose statue stands in a square in Szeged. Tracing the origins of each tune is no easy matter. Even the young Liszt made the mistake of assuming that Gypsy music and Hungarian folk music were the same thing. It was only the careful research of

Bartók and Kodály which set the record straight as to what belonged to each tradition.

The young people – 41 per cent of the population are under 30 – tend to prefer jazz, rock or disco music. They have their own bands, singers and idols, like young people everywhere. Pop concerts are extremely well-attended. Interestingly, though, traditional music is also respected, and there are many *táncház* (dance halls) where you can find both modern and folk dancing on the same evening.

Thousands of young people take part in popular dances, either in performing groups or for fun. A wedding or even a birthday celebration in a family will usually end in a frenetic *csárdás* – the national folk dance whose name derives, appropriately enough, from the word *csárda*, or inn.

Something else that brings the generations together, and reveals another side to the multi-faceted Hungarian character, is laughter. There is a kind of national cult of the humorous anecdote, known as the *vicc*. This comes in at least three varieties: the peasant version, the city version, and the intellectual version. The *pesti vicc* (from Budapest) is regarded by some as a rather plodding form of this mercurial art, but in many ways it is a remarkable social phenomenon. It spreads rapidly, acting as a form of public conscience. There is even a thing called 'viccology' – serious academic research in the subject – which involves careful recording, indexing, comparison and analysis of jokes and tales. Apparently some 3000 new *vicc* appear every 20 years – roughly three per week. The favourite topics are public life, drunkards, mothers-in-law and so on. And yet – another intriguing statistic – only 0.3 per cent of the jokes are at the expense of women. What does this prove? That Hungarian men are exceptionally gallant? (They are inveterate kissers of ladies' hands, even today.) Or that their mothers-in-law are exceptionally lovable? Or is the statistic itself a joke?

The gaiety of the Hungarians should not be taken for granted, however. They are also notorious for their pessimism. Social surveys consistently confirm this, as do some grimly persuasive statistics: Hungary has by far the highest suicide rate in the world, the second or third highest rate of divorce, and half a million alcoholics (out of a population of 10.5 million). A pessimist, according to the Hungarian proverb, is merely an optimist who knows the truth.

Explanations for this black streak in the national character vary. Some say that history is to blame:

A summer's afternoon outside the parliament building in Budapest, with the Danube flowing past (far left).

The 1890s interior of the Hungária café in Budapest, a favourite rendezvous of writers, journalists and actors. Upstairs in the same building, the New York Palace, are the editorial offices of magazines and newspapers.

Kecskemét, the birthplace of the composer Zoltán Kodály, and one of Hungary's most architecturally interesting towns, has many examples of baroque and art nouveau buildings standing side by side.

An image of past and present in Hungary: two peasant women in a street in Budapest. Country people come into town to sell traditional items such as lace, embroidery and dolls to the tourists.

Hungarians tends to contradict this depressing view. Precisely because their language is not international, they are forced to learn other languages, giving them an impressive breadth of culture. They are also noticeably quick-minded and energetic, as well as highly adaptable. And there is that famous sense of humour, evident even in the blackest moments: the writer George Mikes recalls that when the Russians sent their army in to crush the 1956 uprising, 'killing hundreds of innocent citizens, turning the huge guns of their tanks on residential buildings and on crowds and causing devastation and death while proclaiming on the radio that they were coming as friends, Budapest, with its wry humour, commented: "A good thing they're coming as friends. Imagine how they'd behave if they came as enemies".'

Progress

Sixty years ago, Hungary was called 'the country of three million beggars'. Today, while not one of the richer countries of the world, Hungary is certainly far better off than it was before the Second World War. This is partly due to the intensive programme of industrialisation that took place between 1947 and 1965, but it is also due to the sheer hard work and ingenuity of Hungarians themselves. They are ambitious people, desperately keen to improve the quality of their lives. 'Getting by' is one of their specialities: a famous humourist once defined the typical Magyar as the man who enters a revolving door after you but somehow manages to come out first ... Generally, though, they use less mysterious means, such as having two or three jobs. This is similar to what is known as the 'black economy' in other countries.

Women, who make up 45 per cent of the active population, play an important role. With a well-developed system of infant care, including crèches and nurseries, as well as generous maternity leave – three years for either parent – women really are emancipated in Hungary. Working mothers, though, still face the same problems as they do in other countries, with homes to run as well as full-time jobs. And although there is theoretical equality of rights and pay between the sexes, men still tend to hold most senior positions.

In 1968, Hungary introduced the so-called New Economic Mechanism, which was designed to free the economy from the shackles of rigid central planning. With opportunities for private enterprise eagerly taken up, the Mechanism brought a new prosperity to Hungary during the 1970s. Foreign journalists even spoke of a 'Hungarian miracle' of thriving trade under a communist régime. The miracle did not last, however, and the 1980s saw increasing difficulties as the successful balance between a free and controlled economy proved harder and harder to maintain. By 1988, stagnant production, soaring prices, rising unemployment and poverty, and mounting foreign debt left the Hungarian model looking bedraggled. There was still, at least by East European standards, an appearance of wealth – unlike those in Russia, shops in Budapest were filled with goods – but behind the

according to this theory, the Hungarians never quite recovered their confidence after losing the battle of Mohács to the Turks in 1526, and until 1990, lived more or less continuously under foreign oppression; there was then the added humiliation of losing large parts of their territory after the First World War. Others blame the isolating effect of the language, which is unlike any of the languages spoken by their neighbours in Austria, Czechoslovakia, Romania and Yugoslavia, or indeed practically anywhere else in the world. In his book *Hungary, The Art of Survival* (1988), Paul Lendvai wrote, 'Since time immemorial the spirit of the Magyars has wavered between devotion to their mission as founders of the great Kingdom of St Stephen's Crown in the Carpathian Basin, and a deep-rooted fear of extermination – the slow death of a solitary nation without relatives – surrounded by hostile Romanians, Slavs and Germans.'

This may be true, yet personal experience of meeting

apparent normality, crisis loomed. Despite the economic reforms of 1968, Hungarians came to realise that they had the disadvantages of both capitalism and socialism with the advantages of neither.

In February 1989, at the beginning of the reform process which led to the first free elections held in Hungary for more than forty years, a report was published by the historical commission of the Hungarian Socialist Workers Party central committee. This re-examined the events of October-November 1956, and with them Communism itself.

The report broke with the traditional Communist interpretation of the uprising, calling it a 'national independence struggle' instead of a 'counter-revolution'. It went on to say that 'under the Stalin regime, the ideal of international communism was turned into a merciless imperial programme. In the shadow of this endeavour Marxist humanism completely vanished.' Instead came a system founded on 'bloody dictatorship, bureaucratic centralism, fear and retaliation. This became the compulsory model for the social, economic and political transformation of the countries liberated by the Soviet Union from Nazism.' It was a remarkable document, described by *The Independent* newspaper as 'the most damning indictment of the Soviet system ever published in the eastern bloc'.

At the same time, Imre Pozsgay, a leading reformer in the politburo, admitted that the socialist model adopted by Hungary in 1948-9 'had proved to be the wrong path in its entirety'. Now, with the socialist model discredited and the free market all the rage, it remains to be seen whether the damage of those forty years can be reversed, and whether the 'Hungarian miracle' can be repeated.

Festivals and religion

Soon after their arrival in central Europe, the Magyars of the 10th century were to abandon their shamanistic religion in favour of Christianity. This happened under the leadership of King (later Saint) Stephen, the founder of the Hungarian state. In the year 1000, in recognition of his faith, Pope Sylvester II presented Stephen with a crown which became the symbol of the Magyar kings for succeeding generations.

Despite its relative liberalism, the Church tried to prohibit carnivals and dancing, which the people of Hungary have always loved, but which the Church believed to be sinful. The attempt proved vain, and several traditional carnivals dating back to the Middle Ages are still celebrated today.

One of these is the procession of comic and frightening masked figures known as the *busójárás*. The masks represent animals such as bears, horses, storks, goats and bulls, or traditional human characters: the brigand, the old man or woman, the Gypsy, the Turk and the Devil. There are some particularly fearsome figures in the carnival at Mohács, which is said to be a kind of historical exorcism of the defeat suffered here in 1526 at the hands of the Turks. Other carnivals, such as the flower festival at Debrecen, are modern creations,

aimed principally at tourists, though they are pleasant enough all the same.

Many colourful customs survive in Budapest. On New Year's Eve, the streets fill with people throwing confetti to the raucous sound of trumpets. On Easter Monday, young girls are sprinkled with water – to 'keep them fresh'. (These days eau de cologne is used, though once it was ordinary water.) The girls reply by offering painted eggs. This ancient custom symbolises the

The reading room of the Jewish library. Some 600,000 Hungarian Jews died at the hands of the Nazis in the Second World War; today there are about 100,000. The largest synagogue in the world is in Budapest.

renewal of life in spring. At Christmas, children sing around the crib, although Santa Claus has taken over from the golden hen as the bringer of presents.

Ethnographic studies have revealed the existence of many more ancient customs all over Hungary, including the disconcerting *kikolompolás* ('shouting on the roofs'), which is a public denunciation of adultery.

Traditional crafts such as weaving, pottery, wood-carving, furniture-painting and lace embroidery continue to thrive. In some regions, especially in the north, the women still wear the old peasant costumes. These include the great curiosity of white mourning clothes, an ancient custom dating back to pre-Christian times when the souls of the dead were believed to need to be accompanied by a shaman to the world beyond.

Despite these relics of a pagan past, the Church has been a key influence in the culture of Hungary. The conversion of the Magyars to Christianity brought integration with the Western world. The Reformation too had a powerful effect, particularly in the east of the country, with the Reformed College (Református Kollégium) of Debrecen providing a focus for progressive social and educational thinking.

Besides the Reformed College at Debrecen, there are other historic religious foundations: the Rabbinical School in Budapest, the only such institution in central and eastern Europe; the Benedictine Abbey of Pannonhalma; the Christian Museum at Esztergom, with its magnificent collection of altarpieces, tapestries, sculptures and objects in gold, silver and ivory; and many others.

Roman Catholicism remained the established religion in Hungary until quite recently. In fact, the formal separation of Church and State occurred only in 1964, when an agreement was reached with Rome whereby the State pays for the restoration and maintenance of listed religious buildings and subsidises clerical salaries.

The people

Hungarians are early risers. Many offices open at eight in the morning, although the start of the working day in the various institutions and commercial enterprises is deliberately spaced out so as to minimise congestion on the roads. After about 11 o'clock in the evening, the traffic in Budapest thins out considerably, but the city does not go totally to sleep. The Moulin Rouge and Maxim – two of Budapest's most famous cabarets – open their doors at 11, and the Non Stop Show at the Hotel Thermal on Margaret Island caters for even the most chronic insomniacs with entertainment until dawn.

One of the pleasures of visiting Hungary is meeting the people. There are no tourist ghettoes: everywhere there are real communities, with warm and hospitable inhabitants always happy to make contact with passing strangers – particularly those from Western Europe. The Hungarians are famous for their openness, and for their gift with languages. Communication is never a problem. You will also find that they are a highly cultured people, who go to the cinema and theatre a lot, read books and literary magazines, and take a highly informed interest in politics. It now appears that Hungarians, after all the trials of their thousand-year history, have grasped their chance of achieving democracy, pluralism and freedom.

Originating in India, Gypsies are thought to have come to central Europe in either the 13th or 14th century. Their music has been the cornerstone of Hungarian social life ever since.

Poland

This most tenaciously patriotic of nations is also one that defies
easy definitions. Because its frontiers have so often been drawn
and redrawn – and there have been periods when it ceased to exist
at all as an independent state – Poland is difficult to pin down
geographically. Yet few countries have such a strong sense of
national character. Visitors are struck by the vitality of the Poles,
their spirit of enterprise and their ability to adapt to different
circumstances. These qualities sustained the Poles in their fight to
preserve their traditions under the Communist tyranny, and continue
to do so as they come to terms with the post-Communist order.

Previous page:
Plain and water, horse and peasant ... four of the age-old elements of the Polish landscape. The setting here is Mazury, a region of lakes whose limpid waters have been spared the industrial pollution that afflicts so many of Poland's waterways.

The round felt hat worn by the old man (right) marks him unmistakably as a Górale, one of the mountain people from the south of Poland. As most Poles live on the plains, they are fascinated by the mountains and the Górale, who live in the Beskids, Tatras and Bieszczady ranges of the Carpathian Mountains. To this day, a few Górale men still wear the full traditional costume (below) of felt hat, braided woollen jersey, embroidered trousers, axe-headed cane and, in winter, a sheepskin cape.

Most Catholic and Tenacious Nation

Ever since the Chieftain Mieszko set up the first Polish kingdom 1000 years ago, the Poles have been seeking a secure living space. Mieszko, founder of the Piast dynasty, established his authority over the Slav tribes of the mid-Vistula basin around 960 BC, and made Gniezno his capital. The first Christian prince of these hitherto pagan plains, he chose to give his allegiance to the Pope taking baptism in 966, and from that day to this the history of the Poles has been a struggle to preserve their state against encroachment – by their German (and for centuries Catholic) neighbours to the west and the Russian Orthodox and pagan hordes to the east.

For the Poles the problem is that there are few natural and clearly defined frontiers on the plains of their homeland. Although the Baltic Sea borders the north and the Carpathian Mountains the south, what of the west and east? Why does the western frontier lie on the Oder and Neisse rivers rather than the Warta? And why does the eastern border follow much of the Bug river rather than the more eastern Duna and Berezina? There were centuries of conflict, of expansion and withdrawal – including over 100 years (1815-1918) during which independent Poland disappeared altogether – before the country found itself within reasonably secure frontiers. Even this was achieved at the dictates of Stalin rather than the Poles, at the end of the Second World War – a war that cost Poland six million lives and left another three million dispersed in exile.

Like its border history, the country's weather is somewhat uncertain, varying between the rigours of an extreme continental climate and the softer influence of the western winds. Generally, the seasons stand out in sharp contrast to one another, but there are also sudden changes that abruptly melt the January snow on Warsaw's streets, or drive in icy north winds to chill the May Day festivities. Two regular features are the ten or so days of prematurely spring-like weather that briefly warm the country in mid-March, and the gloriously soft and golden Indian summer that often lasts until the end of October. Another oddity is the Polish national time, which follows Western rather than Eastern Europe. So because sunrise is an hour or more ahead of Greenwich Mean Time, in winter dusk falls at three o'clock in the afternoon and in summer it is light by about two o'clock in the morning.

Daybreak in the country

The Polish countryside, almost entirely made up of plains, is at its most appealing in the morning. In spite of its lack of physical variety, generations of peasants

A peasant woman armed with a pitchfork raises one of the small hayricks that dot the mountain landscape of the south in June.

Dense pinewoods cover the sharply rising slopes of the Tatra Mountains. This beautiful region is a favourite weekend spot for people from Cracow, who come here to escape the hustle of the city.

Horses still play their part at the heart of Poland's rural life. Not only working farm horses, either. Some of the world's finest Arab thoroughbreds are reared on Poland's lush plains.

have moulded a pleasantly pastoral landscape. Until the Second World War, Poland was predominantly rural, and it is still in the countryside – even after the havoc wrought by the war and the ugly modern rebuilding that followed it – that you catch a glimpse of the age-old Poland. Fields bordered by wooden fences alternate with forests and woods. Horses draw light carts along the lanes, where in autumn low hayricks rise on either side from the early morning mist that clings to the mown fields, and in small orchards around wooden farmhouses, the fruit trees are wrapped in straw to protect them from the frost.

Nearby a young girl, her shawl slung over her head, hangs out some washing to catch the sun's first warmth, while beyond her a couple of peasants wielding forks spread manure from a cart silhouetted on the crest of a small rise.

At the entrance to the nearest village, a park dotted with ancient lime trees shields an old mansion – one of thousands all over Poland where, only 100 years ago, the nobility accounted for ten per cent of the population. More like manor houses than grand country houses in the style of England or France, the mansions are generally low-set with one, or at most two, storeys. Round the columned porch that shelters the main entrance, wreaths of Virginia creeper or honeysuckle clamber over the brick walls. Today, such places are likely to be hotels, the weekend retreats of journalists' associations, holiday centres for steelworkers or the village's cultural centre. Since the overthrow of the Communist regime in 1989, some of them have been

bought back by their former owners, though the houses have long since been shorn of the estates that once supported them.

Not far away, just outside the village, there is a stone-walled cemetery with a wrought-iron gateway. Inside, all is in perfect order. Trees growing among the tombs create green vaults over the pathways, and bunches of bright flowers stand out in front of the grey headstones, with candles beside them cradled in small cups of melted wax. A visit to the cemetery to take fresh flowers and candles is a standard ritual after Mass each Sunday. The slender-towered brick or wooden church, meanwhile, sometimes stands alongside the cemetery, though more often it rises in the centre of the village.

Even under the Communists, most of Poland's peasant farmers owned their own land. Even so, like everyone else, they have had some difficulty in adapting to the rigours of the post-Communist economic situation.

Still a common sight on Polish roads is the heavy horse-drawn cart, or furmanka. *Where many side roads are little more than gravelled tracks, the sturdy horse-drawn vehicle often has the edge on the motorised one.*

The cart and the car

It is Sunday. In a little village in the east of Poland, somewhere between Pulawy and Lublin, a group of heavy open carts, *furmanki*, drawn by sturdy horses with flowing white manes sets off along the road out of the village. Seated inside each cart is a family on the way home from the High Mass of midday, the *suma*. Winter is drawing to its close and the snow, which for several months has been regularly ploughed off the tarmacked main roads, now lingers only in a few patches. The carts make their way steadily, and a few impatient motor cars – mostly the ubiquitous Fiat Polski 126 – carry relatives and friends on a visit from Warsaw.

One such group turns off the main road down an unpaved lane that the melting snows have turned into little more than a mud track. The *furmanka* keeps up its steady pace. In a field beside the lane the first green sprouts of winter wheat, sown in October, are beginning to push up among the remaining pockets of snow. The lane takes a sharp left-hand turn through a small pine wood bordered with birch trees. The gravel-strewn surface of the lane is gouged here into two long ruts, and the son-in-law's Fiat 126, which until now has been leading the way, gets stuck. The *furmanka* overtakes it, the occupants jeering good-naturedly at the unfortunate driver. He finally extricates himself and the procession continues for another mile or two between fields whose

The plain of Greater Poland is the traditional heart of the country. Once it was one of the great granaries of Europe but, having lost what is today called Western Ukraine to the former Soviet Union under the Yalta Agreement, Poland now has to import wheat.

wooden fences are a soggy, rotting green from years of wet and snow. Eventually, they reach another lane leading to their farm, which was the farmer's private property even during the Communist regime, under which 70 per cent of Poland's agricultural land was privately owned.

A dog of indeterminate breed scampers out from one of the farmyard buildings. Its barking arouses a gaggle of geese and ducks which appear round a corner, necks erect and wings flapping. The *furmanka* stops in front of a large wooden barn, the *stodowa*. This was once thatched, but the last time the roof had to be repaired the straw was replaced with tarred felt. The thatch has also gone from what was once the farmhouse – a one-storey building whose walls are covered with upright planks of wood. In the old days it was painted a delicate pastel blue, but that has long since faded and no one has bothered to repaint the old building since it was relegated to use as a workshop.

It is the new, brick farmhouse alongside that now receives all the attention ... new, but not yet finished. The outside is still unpainted, and as yet there is no balustrade round the small concrete balcony. Will the family ever manage to finish it? The problem is finding

the materials, time and money. In the meantime, plastic sheets cover heaps of unused bricks and rolls of zinc. They cannot get the cement they need to lay bricks for the cowshed and stable, so the now unharnessed horse goes into the old wooden one to rejoin the farm's other horse and four cows. The low building of breeze blocks and corrugated iron, recently completed, is the pig sty; the *kurnik* (hen coop), *ubikacja* (outside toilet) and well complete the furnishings of the yard.

The farmer, wearing felt boots and a heavy flannel smock, takes off his cap as he enters the house, and the women remove their woollen shawls. Today being

One of the last places in Poland to keep alive the old peasant traditions of house decoration is Zalipie in the Carpathian foothills south of Sandomierz and Cracow. House walls inside and out, as well as every kind of kitchen and household utensil, are painted with brightly coloured patterns of flowers and birds.

Embroidery is still a popular art in Poland. Village women embroider banners for religious processions, blouses for their daughters, and shawls and tablecloths for special occasions. Sometimes they come into the cities to sell their wares from door to door.

Sunday, they have exchanged their weekday rubber boots and long woollen leggings for leather ankle boots and tights, and instead of the usual thick linen skirts and layers of knitted jerseys, they are wearing dresses. Once inside, they make straight for the coal stove that is one of the large living room's few furnishings, along with the table, the television, the dresser, the fridge and the pictures of the Virgin Mary and the Pope hanging on the walls.

The meal for which the family has gathered, and which was prepared earlier that morning, will be eaten later at four o'clock. It is the *obiad*, the principal meal of the day. Meanwhile, the plates of ham (*szynka*), some smoked loin of pork (*poledwica*) and homemade pâté laid out on the table's waxed cloth are no more than snacks to go with the vodka that everyone drinks from small glasses emptied at a gulp, followed immediately by larger glasses of water. The cold meats and pâtés are cut into morsels and eaten on small slices of bread. There are also mushrooms pickled in vinegar (*gaski*) and pickled gherkins.

At four o'clock, the serious eating begins. This starts with soup, an obligatory highlight of the *obiad*. Today it is *krupnik*, which contains barley flour and pieces of boiled meat. Because there are so many visitors from the city, the farmer's wife has roasted a goose (*ges*), but normally it would be a duck or chicken. Accompanying the bird are *ziemniaki* – the inevitable potatoes – and

In the traditional peasant home, the kitchen range was the focal point and chief ornament of the living room, as well as being the cooking stove. Sadly, such glorious arrays of colour are becoming a thing of the past – today the fridge and the modern cooker are found nearly everywhere.

cauliflower served with melted butter and breadcrumbs. The meal is rounded off with a yeast cake bought from the baker and a *kompot* – dried fruit, apples, pears and red *sliwki* (plums) all floating in a thick pink syrup that is drunk after the fruit has been fished out. During the meal the feasters also drink strong tea, poured into tall glasses in metal holders and diluted with hot water. As night falls, it is time for the guests to start for home, their cars laden with provisions from the farm or from roadside stalls: apples, pears, vegetables, chickens, ducks. Later in the year there will be strawberries, red and black currants, tomatoes and cucumbers. And from July, village urchins will sell baskets of mushrooms collected that morning – fleshy ceps, chanterelles and milky-green *rydze*. The cars are also overflowing with bunches of heather and branches of elder and hawthorn, which the city-dwellers will use to help to brighten their drab apartments.

Stucco or concrete?

As the returning weekenders reach the edge of Warsaw, the traffic increases. Factories loom on either side of the road, then bleak grey rows of high-rise apartment blocks with their naked slabs of raw concrete or breeze blocks – similar to those spread out around all Poland's major cities. Cars turn off towards them down bumpy access roads and are occasionally brought to a halt at level crossings. Waiting for the train to pass, the occupants may spy the lights of the enormous, hideous Palace of Culture and Science, that rises in the centre of Warsaw as a monument to the Stalinist era. Nowadays it is used for just about everything except culture, since nobody knows how to get rid of it.

Poland's city suburbs are one of the less fortunate aspects of a remarkable drive to rebuild the country after the Second World War. For, of all the nations devastated by the war, it was probably Poland that

Housewives bargain with peasant women who have come in to Pultusk, a small town north of Warsaw, with precious loads of tomatoes and vegetables. In the background, the neo-classical fronts that surround the market square are reconstructions. As with so many Polish towns a good 70 per cent of Pultusk was destroyed during the war.

For city dwellers in Poland, finding supplies of food is a never-ending activity. At weekends they descend on family and friends in the country to stock up on eggs, vegetables and meat, which are cheaper there. Peasants who bring their produce to the cities are assured of a good market.

suffered more than any other. Its human losses included, for example, the extermination of three million Jews, most of whom died in notorious Nazi death camps such as Auschwitz (Oswiecim), near Cracow. In addition, 14,000 Polish officers, taken prisoner by the Russians, were executed in the Katyn Forest. As so often in the past, the Poles were caught between two fires, and once again they fought back with incredible bravery. The rising of the Jews of the Warsaw Ghetto in 1943, and later the doomed struggle of the Polish Home Army – fighting overwhelming German forces to the death through the ruins and sewers of Warsaw, while the Russian 'liberating' forces paused on the far bank of the Vistula – stand among the greatest legends of the war. In other parts of the world, soldiers, sailors and airmen of the Free Polish Forces fought equally gallantly to bring about an Allied victory – in the Battle of Britain, at Tobruk, Alamein and Cassino, and in dozens of other similar campaigns.

As for Poland's physical landscape, meanwhile: the fighting left it little more than a heap of rubble, with almost all town and city centres either flattened or gutted. How, then, to rebuild them? The authorities were determined on one thing: not just to build new towns on the ruins of the old, but to reconstruct as far as possible what had been there before. It was an extraordinary enterprise. The tiniest fragments of old buildings were collected from the debris, identified, indexed, and then stored until the time came for restoration. What survived of national and local archives was carefully sifted through, leaf by leaf, for evidence of how particular buildings and streets used to look. At the same time, old paintings were pored over for further hints.

The gigantic task took several decades until in 1978 – a symbolic crowning point – the old royal palace in Warsaw was re-opened. Razed by the Nazis until not one stone was left on top of another, it has now been entirely reconstructed down to the tiniest stucco decorations over its chimney-breasts.

This is how the Renaissance houses and palaces and baroque churches of Warsaw's Stary Miasto (Old Town) were reborn, along with the old merchant homes of Gdansk's Dlugi Targ (Long Market) square, the historic centre of Poznan and more than 100 other towns and cities across Poland. Two jewels had miraculously

escaped the destruction: Cracow and Sandomierz. In the 16th century they had been the two most beautiful cities in the kingdom; today, ironically, they are in urgent need of rescue from the decrepitude that time and pollution have wrought.

The cost of reconstruction

But this heroic effort to rebuild the nation involved a cost. Poland's new Communist rulers were determined to remodel the country according to the Soviet pattern. The nationalisation of agriculture and industry was coupled with grandiose investment projects and wasteful management of the economy. The cost of living soared; the political preferences of the population were ignored and the secret police became all-powerful. Admittedly, the country's industrial expansion was, on the face of things at least, impressive. The post-war settlement brought the whole of the rich coalfield of Silesia in the south-west within the Polish borders – after over two centuries in which it had been shared with Austria and Prussia. Output from that expanded hugely, as did a variety of heavy industries: steel-making, shipbuilding and heavy engineering. But industrial progress also brought some of the worst environmental despoliation and air pollution in Europe.

At the same time, while the centres of the cities were restored to their old glories, rather less attractive new towns were sprouting from bare fields around their perimeters. The pressure from people moving into the cities from the country, from businesses anxious to set up new factories, from members of the new Communist

élite demanding weekend villas, was enormous. And the resources were, quite simply, lacking. To find a sack of cement, bricks, timber, taps and other materials became an all-consuming struggle in which no holds were barred. People in positions of influence shamelessly pulled strings to get what they wanted; those who knew how to plaster and solder made it their career, or a lucrative second job. The authorities raised the skeletons of buildings, leaving others to put in the finishing touches as best they could.

The results were hardly encouraging. Polish homes are tiny by Western standards. The rule was – and still is – approximately ten square yards per person. Young couples, unless they are extremely lucky, have to wait as long as 12 years before they can get their own flat, and this remains the case even after the demise of Communism. Life is lived cheek by jowl with others, yet none of these constraints have succeeded in damping the essential conviviality of the Poles, for whom hospitality and the pleasure of meeting people (*spotkanie*) – as well as the pleasures of the table – are prime virtues. Far from shutting themselves up within their few square feet of privacy, the inhabitants of Warsaw, Poznan, Lódz and other cities remain remarkably ready to open their homes to relatives, friends and even passing strangers. Meals, in particular, are important occasions, from the early morning

Pigeons and people gather among the grey, melting snows of Cracow's central market square, in front of the 16th-century Cloth Hall. Cracow was the capital of the Polish kingdom from 1320 to 1596, and is still one of the country's foremost cultural centres. Outstanding buildings include the royal castle of Wawel (built by Casimir the Great in the 14th century), a 15th-century university and the Church of the Virgin Mary with one of Europe's most beautiful altarpieces; as well as active café-theatres and small art galleries.

Devoted reconstruction, stone by stone, is responsible for this glorious housefront in Warsaw's Rynek Starego Miasta (Market of the Old Town). Following the Warsaw Uprising of mid-1944, the city was systematically and brutally razed by the Nazis. After the war the citizens set to with one accord to restore it to as much of its former glory as possible.

One of the hard realities of Polish life was the food kolejka *(queue). Although the market economy, introduced in 1989, has improved the supply of food to some extent, it has also resulted in huge price rises. So the simplest necessities take a daunting bite out of the average worker's wages.*

sniadanie, or breakfast – bread, ham, sausages, eggs and hot, strong tea – gulped down before clocking in at the factory at six o'clock to the mid-morning snack (*drugie sniadanie*); from the afternoon *obiad* after work at 2.30 to the light evening supper, or *kolacja*. If guests are around, no matter how dire the country's plight, people will somehow find some food to place before them – *Postaw sie a zastaw sie* (Put up a good show, even if you have to run into debt) runs an old Polish maxim.

Getting together the provisions for these meals was once a daily anguish, consuming huge amounts of both time and money, that only the peasants in the country were spared. Although queueing is now generally speaking a thing of the past, prices are appallingly high in an economy where pay is rarely able to keep pace with ever-spiralling inflation.

As a result, the lucky dollar-holders are the newly rich, those who have taken advantage of the change in regime to set up lucrative import-export businesses. There are also the emigrés who have come home since 1989, carefully keeping their principal bank accounts in the West.

In fact, these Poles of the 'diaspora' – in London, Paris, New York, Chicago, Brazil, Canada, Australia

The first shots of the Second World War were fired at Gdansk, then known as Danzig. This old Baltic port, like Warsaw more or less completely reconstructed after the war, also saw some of the first shots in Poland's fight for freedom from the Communists. It was here in August 1980 that Solidarity was born.

and Israel – always kept close ties with their homeland, even under the Communists. On summer evenings it is a common sight to see groups of American Poles sitting in the gardens of Chopin's birthplace at Zelazowa Wola on the outskirts of Warsaw, listening with tears in their eyes to the strains of one of his études. This romantic scene has distinctly practical implications: for years, these emigrés will almost certainly have been propping up the finances of brothers, sisters and cousins who stayed behind.

They are part of the global network of Polish solidarity, under which Poles have for centuries been ready to try their fortunes abroad in order to assure the living standards of their relatives at home. In recent decades countless Polish doctors in Africa, architects in Paris, technicians in Germany, construction workers in the Middle East and coal miners everywhere, have been earning their families the benefits of hard currency.

God save Poland

The Catholic church has a unique place in Polish life. For 1000 years it has held the key to the nation's sense of cultural identity and historic role.

As Catholics the people have always regarded themselves as the easternmost bastion of Europe – their destiny to hold back the Asian hordes of Tatars, Turks and Russians. It was partly this sense of a divine mission that inspired the Polish kingdom in its years of greatest glory, when its frontiers extended as far east as Kiev and Smolensk.

In more recent years it was the Catholic church, symbolised above all by the Polish Pope John Paul II, that kept alive the Polish spirit of national pride and resistance to the Communist dictatorship. Church leaders encouraged and supported Solidarity – the first free (that is, not state-controlled) trade union in post-war Eastern Europe, founded in 1980 – and in 1984 the church provided one of Solidarity's best-known martyrs: Father Jerzy Popieluszko, an ardent supporter of the union, who was kidnapped, beaten, strangled and thrown in to a reservoir by agents working for the authorities.

Indeed, it is in church that Poles, young and old alike, feel most Polish. Congregations are large every Sunday, and on the great feast days such as Easter, Corpus Christi and All Saints', they spill out onto the surrounding streets and squares. As well as the nationwide festivals, there are others associated with the different regions. Each year on December 4, for example, the miners of Silesia celebrate *Barburka*, the day of St Barbara, patron saint of miners. On special feast days, as many as half a million converge on Czestochowa in the south, a city overlooked by the Jasna Gora (Hill of Light) Monastery, founded in 1382. Its chief treasure is the Black Madonna, a Byzantine painting of Our Lady of Czestochowa, said to have miraculous powers.

The fervour of these great religious occasions, the flower-bedecked altars, the processions, the precious reliquaries, the candles and incense, the chanting choirs of children and surpliced young priests, all combine to bring the Catholic faith vividly into the heart of everyday life. It is hardly surprising to learn that 95 per cent of Poles profess to be devout Catholics.

Religious festivals are also family occasions, when parents, children, grandchildren, uncles, aunts and cousins can look forward to several days together. Most important of all is Christmas, for which festivities begin with the *wigilia* (vigil) of Christmas Eve. One of the *wigilia*'s highlights is the meal of 12 meatless dishes eaten before going to Midnight Mass. These must, by tradition, include a carp dish, so the housewife almost certainly spends hours that day queuing in the cold outside the fishmonger's. The carp may be lightly sautéed, poached and served in jelly, or poached in wine with herbs. Herring is another traditional favourite, though increasingly hard to find.

There may also be salmon (*losos*), smoked eels (*wegorz*), *bigos* (sour cabbage with wild mushrooms, instead of meat, on this occasion) and dried mushrooms. Accompanying the main dishes will be noodles,

Gulls gather round a solitary, out-of-season visitor to the Baltic coastal resort of Sopot. The characteristic wicker beach chairs in the background are provided with large hoods to protect their occupants from the wind.

potatoes, *pierogi* (dumplings), pickled pears, plums and cucumber and, of course, plenty of vodka. Before sitting down at table, the guests break up small wafers of unleavened bread and hand them to each other. After the meal they head for church, where the air is thick with the mingled smells of vodka, candles and incense.

Easter is the next most important family occasion. On Easter Saturday families take baskets of food to be blessed by the priest. Each of the basket's contents is symbolic of well-being: sausages, bread, salt, pepper and hand-painted eggs. On Easter Day the important meal is lunch. First everybody eats one of the eggs, then they all tuck into numerous different kinds of pâté, sausage and meat.

The church plays a prominent role in the milestones of life: birth, marriage and death. The elaborate festivities surrounding a traditional marriage (*wesele*) involve a good deal more than the religious ceremony itself. Weddings are most spectacular in the country, where festivities may last two or even three days. On leaving the church the couple visit the local photographer while everybody else heads for the reception. The guests include the entire family (in its most extended sense) and the family's friends – probably more than 100 people in all – and they must be royally entertained. A pig is killed for the occasion and

A priest's legs and robes can be seen beneath a portable confessional at Czestochowa during the annual summer pilgrimage in honour of Poland's protectress, the Black Virgin. Pilgrims gather from all over the country for the festival, which has long been a patriotic as well as a religious one.

countless dishes prepared at home. Musicians play popular tunes, and the vodka flows. After the feasting, dancing goes on until dawn. Then the revellers snatch a few hours sleep before the festivities begin again.

In the towns and cities, the festivities tend to be a little less elaborate. Even so, the main celebrations last well into the night and usually until dawn the next morning – the family generally hires the local cultural centre for the occasion. If the party goes on the next day, it will probably be for the inner family circle only. The numbers may be smaller than for a country wedding, but the guests still usually manage to get through plenty of food and drink – and as in the country drunken brawls are not unknown.

Old-fashioned courtesy

Polish women have to be resourceful; in spite of their devoutness, they are also formidably free-thinking. During the presidential election campaign of 1990 the popular candidate, now the president, was Lech Walesa, the former electrician and heroic leader of the free trades union Solidarity. Many women were alarmed when Walesa espoused the church's conservative position on abortion and divorce. In towns and cities particularly, women frequently gave the Solidarity candidate a distinctly frosty reception.

Fashion is another dominant interest. Walking down Nowy Swiat, the great thoroughfare of central Warsaw, you are immediately struck by the inventiveness of the women's clothes which the first days of sunshine have brought into the open. For sheer originality, Warsaw fashion can claim to rival that of Paris, Milan or Tokyo, and the state-owned Moda Polska, the driving force behind local fashion, is a notable success story. It exports clothes to Germany, Scandinavia and Britain as well as throughout Eastern Europe – though the

Not even a thick snowfall can deter the crowds from gathering for the Mystery of the Passion – the Easter celebration at Kalwaria Zebrzydowska near Cracow – as they have for 300 years. Monks and local peasants join forces to re-enact the events of Christ's Passion along a route that is said to be almost exactly like the original one from Jerusalem to Calvary.

Crowds at Lowicz celebrate the Corpus Christi festival with particular fervour as they chant the ancient canticles, the older people garbed in traditional costume. Throughout Poland, the festival is honoured by processions of local people carrying banners and statues of the Virgin.

At Nowy Targ in the foothills of the Carpathians, as everywhere else in Poland, the influence of the church reaches all corners of life. The village priest – who in Communist times was often one of the chief spokesmen against the regime – still wields enormous power in moulding people's opinions and attitudes.

emphasis on export means that few Polish women are able to enjoy its products.

No matter – Polish women show the same ingenuity in dress that they show in finding food for the family table. Recent years have seen a boom in small fashion boutiques opening in smart shopping areas, and in individual dressmakers and designers operating from backstreet workshops. Their products are strikingly up to date, even by Western standards, and also expensive. Even more expensive is the clothes market at Rembertow on the outskirts of Warsaw, where all the cherished appurtenances of the Western lifestyle are available for those who can afford them: German leather boots from Berlin, Italian pullovers and American jeans. For the less fortunate, it is a question of simply making your clothes yourself. As a result, the fashion parade of Polish streets reveals an individual flair – as well as taste – that is often lacking in the West.

Another feature of Poland that is frequently lacking in the West is the old-fashioned courtesy with which men treat women, despite a widespread and growing equality of opportunity for women. There is an attractive, stately charm in the way a Polish man greets a woman by kissing her hand. Men always give way to women at doors, and no rendezvous is complete without the man's proffered bunch of flowers.

Flowers are always plentiful. Flower shops stay open until late in the evening, and the business of growing the flowers is so important that not even the Communist authorities ever dared to bring it under state control, so it has always flourished. Greenhouses are spread out in the fields around most towns and cities, and many of their owners are numbered among the millionaires of the *inicjatyva priwatna*.

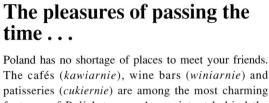

The pleasures of passing the time . . .

Poland has no shortage of places to meet your friends. The cafés (*kawiarnie*), wine bars (*winiarnie*) and patisseries (*cukiernie*) are among the most charming features of Polish towns. An assistant behind the counter, wearing rope-soled espadrilles provided by the management, is often ready for a lengthy chat, even if sometimes making a great show of being rushed off her feet. Lining the glass shelves in front of her are arrays of whatever is available at the moment – cakes (*sernik, kremówka, tort, szarlotka*) or savouries such as herrings prepared in cream, beetroot salad and sardines on rye bread. Before entering, you leave your coat with the ancient pensioner or rather tired-looking matron of the *szatnia*, or cloakroom. Inside, the small tables each have a lamp casting a dim glow through a tinted red or brown shade. It is the perfect place to enjoy a leisurely,

A fiddler entertains crowds in the old town of Kazimierz on the Vistula, south-east of Warsaw. The drab uniformity demanded by the Communist regime left its leaden mark on much of Poland's architecture, but it was unable to stifle the old folk traditions.

Here dressed for a local harvest festival, this girl has the long blonde hair, fine nose and high cheekbones of a classic Polish beauty. Later, she is more likely to be seen in jeans dancing the night away in the village disco.

intimate chat and to forget the thousand difficulties and harassments of everyday life.

At night, people while away the hours in student clubs or the club houses of professional associations. Drink is a little scarce in the many discos, but live bands playing jazz, pop or rock and the latest records from London, Berlin and Stockholm make up for that. Records are the fastest-selling Western product. Hardly is the latest album released in the West before it is on sale (at a premium) in Warsaw and other cities. Friends swap albums, tape them at home and then pass them on to other friends. These are the recordings they dance to when they go back to their tiny flats after the discos have closed. Later, at about two or three o'clock in the morning, the hostess (*pani domu*) may hand round bowls of *barszcz*, a hot soup, and *pierogi* of meat, thus helping to prolong the fun. Finally people start dialling 919, the radio-taxi and the only prudent way to get home in a country where the police are always ready to pounce on drivers with their breathalysers.

With all these pleasant pastimes – visiting friends and relatives, discussing and arguing, making plans for the future – there is still time for the other great Polish passion: reading. As well as the works of their own writers, the Poles read widely in American, British, French, Italian, German and Swedish literature, and many of the contemporary works are translated into Polish before they appear in other European languages. In Communist times, despite the best efforts of the censors to keep them out, foreign books were one of the few ways the Poles had of finding out what people were thinking and doing in the rest of the world. Even where translations were not available language was rarely a problem, because many Poles have a good knowledge of English, French and German – as well as Russian, though bitter memories of the former Soviet occupation mean that Russian is rapidly becoming a 'forgotten' language in Poland.

Poland's old folk dances are disappearing from many of the villages where they originated, but are being picked up by amateur dance groups in Warsaw, Cracow, Poznan, Wroclaw and other major cities. They perform at national festivals, such as that of July 22, and many groups have made successful foreign tours.

Fishermen enjoy the silence
and tranquillity of the forest
of Bialowieza, straddling the
frontier between Poland and
Belorussia. One of the largest
expanses of forest left in
central Europe, Bialowieza
was a royal hunting ground
from the 15th to the 18th
century. Earlier in this
century it was one of the chief
refuges of the Polish
Resistance to both Soviet and
Nazi invaders. Now it is a
nature reserve.

The Kashub country south of
Gdansk is a world unto itself.
Nobody knows where its
people originated, and their
language is quite distinct
from Polish, or any other Slav
or Germanic tongue. They
also cling tenaciously to their
old ways of life – such as
using nets to trawl the waters
of frozen lakes for a winter
harvest of fish.

A thirst for knowledge has always been a Polish characteristic, even when official publications were deliberately designed to obscure the truth. In fact, the censors were rarely very efficient. Clandestine publications usually managed to circulate, and there were also plays, films and songs that somehow escaped their vigilance or simply overwhelmed them with their abundance. To be fair to the Communists, they did do much to encourage Polish music, cinema and theatre. State backing was given to contemporary composers such as Witold Lutoslawski and Krzysztof Penderecki and to film directors such as Andrzej Wajda and Andrzej Munk. Wadja's war trilogy – *A Generation, Canal, Ashes and Diamonds* – were among a number of outstanding Polish films which went on to achieve international fame.

Caricature and derision, meanwhile, also proved effective in decrying Communist officialdom, and are still used to poke at the authorities on the general plight of the country. 'What's the difference between Poland before the war and Poland now?' asked one old joke. 'Before the war, there were shops with the sign "butcher" outside, and inside there was meat. Nowadays, the same shops have the sign "meat" outside, and inside there's a butcher.'

Back to nature

In summer the Poles head in droves for their beloved countryside. Some spend their holidays in centres belonging to workers' associations; others go camping

Europe's only remaining bison live in the forest of Bialowieza. Most of the original population were killed when the forest was mined during the First World War, but since then a number bred in zoos have been successfully reintroduced.

or take lodgings with peasants. Over the last two decades, more and more families have acquired their own cars, and the annual task of cramming four people along with their equipment for a fortnight's camping into a single Fiat 126 has become something of a national skill.

For most Poles, enjoyment of the countryside is not limited to summertime. Even in the depths of winter, families spend Sundays tramping snowy forest trails, warmly enveloped in fur coats (*kozuch*) and caps (*czapka*), or taking sleigh rides through the glades. But tragically many of these forests are dying. The change of regime has brought into sharp focus the grim reality of pollution. The cost of the Communists' policy of promoting heavy industry at all costs, with scant regard for its effects on the environment, is particularly evident in the region west of Cracow.

This has not diminished the pleasure the Poles take in nature and the outdoors. The first days of spring sunshine in mid-March bring an explosion of life as everyone heads out to enjoy the warmth. By June and then on through the summer, hosts of people are sunbathing in Warsaw's many parks and on the grassy banks of the Vistula. The glorious days of the long, golden autumn (*zlota jesien*) see them trudging through the forests once more, eyes down as they seek out the mushrooms (*gryzyby*) which they will later dry or bottle at home to enliven winter meals.

Hunting is another popular activity, for which members of tightly controlled hunting fraternities have access to the remoter depths of the immense forests of the east. The wild animals abounding in these parts include wild boar, several kinds of deer and even Europe's last-surviving bison.

Some families also enjoy seaside holidays at Baltic resorts such as Sopot or Hel or smaller fishing villages. But they have to be hardy; the water, even in the height of summer, is decidedly chilly, and sunbathers need to be well sheltered by canvas windbreaks. Other outdoor attractions are the mountains of the south, at Zakopane or in the Bieszczady range, especially in autumn when watching the sunset on the golden, forest-covered slopes is an unforgettable experience.

But wherever Poles take their holiday, they must be home for October 31, All Souls' Day. This is another of the great religious festivals. In Warsaw everyone heads for the Powazki Cemetery, where they lay large wreaths of flowers on family tombs and light candles or small lamps. Even after nightfall they stay in the cemetery, strolling along the alleys between the tombs, gathering in groups round the memorials to national heroes and singing patriotic songs. It is a poignant time, expressive of all the tragedies, hardships and yet sheer resilience of the Polish nation. Nowadays, that resilience seems to be needed more than ever as a country ravaged by four decades of Communism seeks to adjust itself to a new way of existence.

The uncertainties of the future were emphasised in 1990 when Lech Walesa was elected president with no more than 38 per cent of the vote. Huge numbers of Poles, having fought so long and hard for their freedom, and now faced with their country's continuing and seemingly insoluble economic problems, had deemed it pointless to exercise their democratic rights.

On November 11, the Poles celebrate the rebirth of the Polish nation after the First World War. The dead are traditionally remembered. People mark the festival with tokens of remembrance for all those who have died down the centuries for the nation's independence. This banner commemorates the Solidarity martyrs of the 1980s.

Romania

As its name suggests, Romania (the ancient Dacia) was one of the heartlands of the Roman Empire. Set in the midst of the Slav world they are a proudly Latin race, with a Latin-based tongue. History has not always treated them kindly. For centuries part of the Turkish Empire, they won their freedom in 1878, but have since endured several tyrannies, notably that of the infamous Nicolae Ceausescu who was finally ousted in 1989. Not even Ceausescu, however, could efface the beauty of a land stretching from the plateaus of Transylvania to the Danube delta with the forested slopes of the Carpathian Mountains slicing it in two.

The greens and distant blues of the Transylvanian landscape are matched by the brilliant colour adorning the houses and people: an almost tropical blue for outside walls and bright shades of red, yellow and purple for peasant women's clothes and embroideries.

On the plains surrounding Bucharest, a peasant woman from the Lake Snagov region prepares seed potatoes for next year's harvest.
Even under Ceausescu, most peasants managed to hang onto small, privately owned patches of ground where they could raise a few crops of their own to supplement their meagre living.

Previous page:
In the Maramures Mountains that stretch north from Transylvania to the Ukrainian border, a family group stands at the entrance to the village churchyard before going to Christmas Mass. Here, as in Transylvania, wood is the chief building material. Even the beautiful local churches, jewels of the region's architecture, are built of wood.

Land of Latin Colour and Tradition

Of all the revolutions in Eastern Europe's year of revolutions – 1989 – Romania's was probably the most dramatic. People throughout the world preparing for the Christmas holidays watched spellbound as the spark of revolt against Nicolae Ceausescu's maverick dictatorship was kindled to a flame, first among the ethnic Hungarians of the west then eastwards across the rest of the country. The unthinkable happened: in the capital Bucharest, crowds long cowed into submission by the brutal efficiency of the Securitate, Ceausescu's secret police, dared openly to boo the dictator as he broadcast an address that was being sent live across the nation. Startled, he hesitated and from then on his fate was sealed. As Christmas passed into the New Year, events moved on at an astonishing pace. Ceausescu and his hated wife Elena attempted to flee the country, but were caught, summarily tried and executed. At the same time, bloody street fighting raged between desperate forces loyal to the Ceausescu regime and the armed forces, who had sided with the revolution. Gradually, the National Salvation Front that had been set up in the first flush of the revolt managed to take control of the situation. The fighting died down and Romania, until then the last bastion of unreconstructed Communism in the former Soviet Bloc, seemed set fair to take its place among the newly free nations of Eastern Europe.

The land in which these extraordinary events took place can justly claim to be among the most beautiful in Eastern Europe. Created from the union of Wallachia in the south and Moldavia in the north during the 19th century, with Transylvania and the Banat added in 1918, Romania encompasses a spectacular variety of scenery. Dominating the country from north to south is the great mountain sweep of the Carpathians, sketching a gigantic arc around to the south-west. Descending from them on either side are regions of hills and high plateaus, that fall away in turn to plains spreading out to the frontiers. These lower lands are extremely fertile. Vines and fruit orchards (apples, pears, cherries, apricots, plums and quinces) clothe the hills and plateaus, and the plains are given over to intensive cereal cultivation.

The Carpathians rise to their highest peak, Moldoveanu (8346 feet) in the Transylvanian Alps, which, along with the famous Iron Gate gorge on the Danube at their south-western end, offer some of the loveliest scenery. On the lower slopes of the mountains there are extensive hardwood forests, which give way to conifers higher up. The forests are interspersed with open stretches of alpine pasture where flocks of sheep graze in summer. Whatever the industrial contamination in the cities on the plains, the air up here is amazingly fresh and pure.

Many of Romania's rivers rise in the Carpathians before tumbling down the mountain-sides to join the Danube. This bounds the country to the south, reaching

Homes are cramped in the villages of the Maramures Mountains. To save space, brightly coloured kitchen utensils are often hung outside under the wide eaves. Small though they are, the wooden houses are well able to withstand the rigours of cold in winter and heat in summer.

the end of its 1770-mile journey eastwards across Europe in the Danube delta on the Black Sea. The delta has a desolate magic: thousands of channels open up narrow passages through beds of giant rushes, while overhead wind-lashed clouds create dramatic skyscapes. Its wealth of plant life and animal life includes wolves, which still roam its marshy wildernesses, and countless species of birds that nest there or pass through as they migrate north or south.

The Romanian people are proud of being a Latin race. They claim descent from the Greco-Dacians, who belonged to the family of the Thracians. After part of Dacia was conquered by the Romans in the 1st century AD, the Dacian and Roman civilisations mingled, a process which resulted in the Romanisation of the Dacians and the birth of the Romanian people. The Romanian language, unlike those of their Hungarian neighbours to the west and their Slav neighbours on all other sides, is recognisably Latin-based. Much of their outlook on life also has a Latin cast – the love of festivals, for example. But as with the rest of Eastern Europe, the dominant national group does not have the country to itself. In Transylvania, and, in particular, the Banat region bordering Hungary, Romanians have for centuries lived alongside ethnic Germans (known variously as Swabians and Saxons) and ethnic Hungarians.

Flocks of pelicans are just one element of the Danube delta's rich wildlife. The huge region of reed jungles, mud flats and maze-like river channels lies at the crossroads of numerous bird migration routes, and in spring and autumn plays host to species as varied as singing swans, polar grebes, glossy ibises and eagles – golden, fishing and sea types. Resident mammals include otters, muskrats, boars and wolves.

Communal effort has been part of the way of life in the Transylvanian Alps for centuries, long before the Communists took over. The mountain people work together in order to make the best of a precarious living. Here, a group of women are chopping away at the thistles and other weeds that regularly invade their alpine pastures.

Wolves still roam the lonelier parts of Romania. Far from being the fearsome creatures of legend, they do not attack humans unless driven by extreme hunger. Wild game, sheep and occasionally cows and horses are their preferred prey. They hunt singly in summer, but in winter gather in packs whose eerie howls can sometimes be heard at night in remote villages.

Memories of Dracula and painted monasteries

Peasants at the market in Radauti, northern Moldavia, use white and coloured rags to display the vegetables and spices they have brought in. The small amounts they have to sell are a poignant testimony to the meagre living of this mountain region, where soils are poor and resources few compared with the rich potential of Romania's southern plains.

One consequence of the variety of landscapes and peoples is an equal variety of building styles. Romanian popular architecture reflects the different building materials, climates and customs of each region. In Transylvania, for example, village homes are usually ample, many-roomed buildings with brick or wooden upper storeys resting on a ground floor of stone. A wide, sun-catching verandah often surrounds the house, and the roof (which may have been in place for 150 years or more) is typically thatched or made of shingle. North of Transylvania, in the Maramures Mountains, wood alone is used often, to wonderful effect; architectural gems include the *biserici de lemn* (wooden

churches), with splendidly carved doorways and slender bell-towers rising as high as 200 feet.

To the south, in the Oltenia region of Wallachia, many villages are dominated by fortified manor houses, *cule*, surrounded by wide verandahs with finely carved pillars. They are one reminder of Wallachia's troubled past as a buffer zone between Christian Europe and the Muslims of the Turkish Empire. Another is the fortification now universally known as Dracula's Castle, perched dramatically on a rocky 1200-foot outcrop above the River Arges. Here, in the 15th-century, Wallachian Prince Vlad Dracul 'the Impaler' – model in part for *Dracula*, author Bram Stoker's vampire – held his court. In Vlad's time no one associated him with Romania's vampire myths; he was certainly, however, a ruthless ruler who fought successfully against the Turks and governed his own people with capricious cruelty. He owed his nickname to his preferred method of dealing with captured enemies – impaling them on a stake to die a slow and agonising death.

Farther east, in the Danube delta and along the Black Sea coast, clay and the abundant stocks of reeds take over as building materials. Clay is used for house walls and the reeds, supported on slender wooden columns, for the thatched roofs. To the north in Moldavia and Bukovina, the brightly coloured frescoes covering the outside walls of some buildings are the most striking feature. A few ordinary houses have them, but the most spectacular are on the famous painted monasteries where the walls blaze forth their medieval visions of the Fall and the Last Judgement.

On the other side of the country, in Transylvania and the Banat, the ethnic Germans and Hungarians each have their own characteristic building styles. Some Germans keep up the old custom of inscribing proverbs in praise of hard work, honesty and hospitality on the fronts of their houses. Another intriguing community, the Szekely (closely related to the Hungarians and speaking a dialect of Magyar), have a special mastery of the art of making fret-saw patterns. Their homes in the eastern Carpathians are covered with delicately sawn traceries that resemble lacework carved in wood.

Socialist man's bleak paradise

If variety and charm are the chief characteristics of Romania's village architecture, the cities are less fortunate. Bucharest was once known as the 'Paris of Eastern Europe' and many of its spacious parks, handsome 19th-century boulevards and terraced cafés and restaurants survive, particularly around the grand thoroughfare of the Calea Victoriei (Victory Road). But

At Sighetu Marmatiei in the Maramures, as in most parts of the country, the women take charge of selling the produce from the family plot or the output of the cooperative. Market days also give the women a chance to catch up on the gossip of neighbouring villages, and even sometimes to arrange marriages for their sons and daughters.

the capital was also the victim of one of the more insane follies of Ceausescu's 24-year tyranny. In an attempt to create a city worthy of the 'New Socialist Man', he had huge swathes of its oldest and most attractive districts (including several 18th-century churches and the Orthodox cathedral) bulldozed to make way for a soulless modern Civic Centre.

This piece of barbarism was just one of the many ill-considered and ill-fated projects launched by Ceausescu, for which the Romanian people had to

Seated on her porch a woman weaves the plain white cloth for others to transform with embroidery. She has no artificial materials or 'high-tech' aids – just the simplest of wooden looms and her own skill and diligence.

Girls and young unmarried women in the Maramures spend years preparing their trousseaux and the household linen they will one day take with them to their new homes. The skills involved in making embroidered covers such as these are passed down from generation to generation, and are part of the region's folk traditions.

Embroidered fabrics, made in Romania's mountain regions, have been much in demand by visiting townspeople and foreign tourists in recent years. This has led to a small economic revolution enabling women to earn some much-needed extra income from their ancient craft.

suffer. The food shortages – common throughout Communist Eastern Europe – were nowhere worse than in Romania, even though it is a comparatively fertile and productive land. The fault lay not so much with the collectivised state farms, as with Ceausescu's insistence that all available food should be exported. This would help to earn the hard currency needed to pay off the debts he had run up with the West during the 1970s. New industry, meanwhile, particularly the chemical plants at Giurgiu in the south, was creating some of the worst pollution in Europe. At the same time, the gradual drying-up of the Ploiesti oil fields north of Bucharest,

together with the scarcity of foreign currency, led to acute fuel shortages. So while the city-dwellers went hungry and breathed contaminated air, they also shivered. Power cuts were a regular part of life, and buildings went unheated even in the snows of winter.

As so often in Eastern Europe, the country people escaped comparatively lightly. The collectivisation of agriculture allowed most peasant families small privately owned plots of land where they could keep a few hens and livestock. But some of them fell prey to another of Ceausescu's mad schemes. In the mid-1980s he embarked on a programme to demolish 6000 villages

Many country weddings still follow age-old rites – such as the mock battle between the escorts of the bride and groom when the young man arrives at his loved-one's home to carry her off. Needless to say, this always ends in victory for the groom's party, and the couple then clamber happily into a horse-drawn cart to make their way to the church.

– described as being 'without perspective' – and replace them with 'agro-industrial complexes'. Many villages were destroyed in this way, but fortunately Ceausescu's fall from power meant that many more were spared.

Traditions that live on . . .

These wild schemes, together with the effects of collectivised agriculture, have taken their toll on Romanian village life. Collective farms, introduced by the Communists and currently abolished, have brought

certain improvements in efficiency – their larger resources allow the purchase of more sophisticated equipment, such as modern tractors and combine-harvesters, for example. But they have also brought a stifling bureaucracy, and have diluted many of the more attractive rural traditions.

Yet although a number of villages have been brutally destroyed and ancient communities uprooted, an extraordinary number of the old ways and traditions continue to thrive. For the Romanians have a truly Latin love of festivals. Over the centuries, all the landmarks of life (baptism, marriage and burial) have accumulated their respective traditions of feasting, singing and dancing, and most survive.

Of all these occasions, a traditional marriage is one of the most spectacular. It follows age-old rituals and involves not just the families of the bride and groom, but numerous *vornici* (godparents) and *colacari* (page boys), friends and relatives ... indeed, the whole village and neighbourhood, from the youngest to the oldest. Preparations start months in advance. Just the making of the specially embroidered banner, the *peana* (literally, 'plume'), that flies from the groom's home on the day of the wedding, will have kept the village's young men and women busy in their spare time for several weeks. They will also have made the groom's embroidered shirt, as well as the veil and small crown worn by the bride. The last-minute preparations are even more intense. From daybreak on the wedding morning, village women are busy combing and plaiting the

bride's hair, putting final touches to her dress and arranging her veil and crown, while a chorus of young girls sings bridal songs.

At midday everybody gathers at the groom's house and the wedding procession forms, headed by the *vornici* and *colacari*, one of whom is carrying the *peana*. For mountain weddings the procession is on foot, but in villages on the plains it will be on horseback, the horses splendidly decked out for the occasion. They make their way to the bride's home, and a ritual tussle follows as the groom pretends to carry her off by force while her family pretend to resist. This over, the whole throng makes its way to the church. After the religious ceremony comes the feasting. Wine starts to flow and the bride and groom do their best to make a clean cut in the huge, round cake, or *colac*. During the meal, they feed each other using the same plate and spoon. Once that has been accomplished to everyone's satisfaction, the dancing begins, many of the dances symbolising the sweetness of married life. Towards the end of the evening, friends crowd round the couple to sing songs full of ribald jokes on married life. Finally, the pair are escorted to the bridal chamber.

They are not allowed to enjoy their privacy for long. Promptly at dawn the next day, the villagers gather under their bedroom window to sing the traditional 'dawn song'. The young wife descends and makes her appearance on the threshold, her hair done up in a simple bun and wrapped in a headscarf to show that she has passed honourably into the ranks of mature women.

It is not only the milestones of people's lives that the Romanians like to celebrate. Each year, the passage of the seasons – seedtime and harvest, the movements of the flocks between their summer and winter pastures – is an excuse for numerous different festivities. These start on an attractively musical note on New Year's Day, when groups of singers make the rounds of villages,

No wedding would be complete without dancing. Formal dancing immediately after the church ceremony is followed by more light-hearted entertainment as friends decked in fantastic costumes and headgear make fun of the couple and their closest kin.

Weddings are great social occasions where family and friends gather from far and wide to renew old friendships and catch up on each others' news. As always in Romania, the colours are splendid, especially in the embroidered jackets and brightly adorned head-scarves worn by the women.

singing *colinde* (special New Year carols) outside houses. Later that evening, young farm hands (*plugarasi*) lead an old, ox-drawn plough (*plugusorul*) from house to house, having decorated both the plough and the oxen horns with branches and flowers. Outside each home they cut a symbolic furrow in the ground while a young boy recites traditional verses wishing health, prosperity and an abundant harvest to the people in the house.

In May, the sheep are taken up to their summer pastures in the mountains. It is the custom for a group of farmers to pool their flocks and jointly engage shepherds for the summer. Before they go, there are a number of rituals to go through. Each farmer measures the amount of milk his flock produces so that, at the end of the summer, he will then know how much of the flocks' joint production of cheese is his due. Next the

Romania's numerous local cultures and traditions, and varied climates and building materials, have given the country a variety of popular architectural styles. This brick-built thatched cottage is typical of Transylvania, as is the wooden fence enclosing the precious plot of land within which produce grown is all the family's own, and need not be shared with any cooperative.

sheep are fumigated to get rid of any ticks and other creatures they may have picked up during the winter. After this everyone can settle down to enjoy the festivities of the *simbra oilor* ('gathering of the sheep') or *masurisul* ('measuring of the milk'). The entire village gets together for a common meal in which various kinds of cheese and yoghurt are the highlights. Darkness falls; the feast has been digested, and the dancing and singing begin, lasting well into the night.

Looking to the future

In view of the excesses of one of Eastern Europe's most unpleasant Communist dictatorships, the continuance of all these traditions is a striking testimony to the staying power of the Romanians. It is a quality that has stood them in good stead, for Ceausescu's tyranny was by no means the first they have endured. In this century alone, Romania has suffered the repressive rule of King Carol II in the 1930s, the Fascist-style terror tactics of the Iron Guard in the same decade and during the Second World War the Nazi-backed dictatorship of Marshal Antonescu.

The popular revolution of December 1989 overthrew the dictatorial regime, opening up prospects for the re-introduction of democracy, of the multi-party system and for Romania's full reintegration into the political and cultural life of Europe. Meanwhile, Romanians continue to rely on their Latin zest for living. This has carried them through many past upheavals and provides some refuge from the troubles of the present.

In Sugatag in the far north of Romania, some villagers have slipped away from the boisterous revels of a wedding feast to a quiet spot where they can concentrate on a game of cards.

Bulgaria

Bulgaria first emerged as an independent state in AD 681 and, under a succession of khans and kings, became one of the foremost powers in Eastern Europe, before suffering a 500-year eclipse as part of the Ottoman Empire. Modern Bulgaria won its freedom from Turkey in the 1870s and, like the rest of Eastern Europe, revolted against Communist tyranny in 1989. Now it is slowly finding its place in the new world order. It has much to offer: fertile land, remarkable wines, Black Sea beaches, rugged mountains and beautiful monasteries.

Previous page:
With the summer festivities in full swing, a young girl puts the finishing touches to the headdress she has concocted for the occasion. Bulgarians have a passion for tradition, and always enjoy an opportunity to assert their national identity.

Every region has its own variation on the costume worn for traditional

Bulgarian dances. The basic costume is the same, the unvarying feature being the women's wide-sleeved blouses.

Cobbled lanes are still the norm in Bulgaria's mountain villages, where life continues at the age-old pace. In the Rila and Pirin Mountains of the south-west, in particular, many villages preserve ancient craft traditions.

The Balkans' Forgotten Land

A small, 12th-century gem of a church lost in a grove of cypress trees at Boyana in western Bulgaria in a way emblemises the country as a whole. Though not far from the capital Sofia, the church lies well off the beaten track, and the weeds pushing up between its paving stones bear witness to the neglect of decades. Bulgaria itself, tucked into an eastern corner of the Balkan peninsula, is, as far as the outside world is concerned, the most neglected of the Balkan lands.

The Boyana church interior was revolutionary in its time. Here in 1253, an unknown local master broke with the canons of the Byzantine tradition of painting, by which saints and biblical figures were depicted more or less uniformly with large black eyes and set expressions of piety. Instead, the Boyana frescoes show figures who are recognisably men and women as well as saints; they have an earthy solidity and individuality rare for the period. In the same way the Bulgarian people have regularly managed to break free of their bonds and strike out on their own.

Like most Balkan countries, Bulgaria comprises a mixture of peoples. More than 85 per cent are Slav Bulgarians, themselves the result of a mingling of races in the 5th to 7th centuries AD, when native tribes, Slavs and the Proto-Bulgarians – invaders from the Caucas and the Volga basin, probably related to the modern Turks (though new research actually suggests they may have been Slavs) – came together. Blending fairly readily with the Bulgarians are small numbers of Romanians, Greeks, Macedonians, Tatars and Armenians. Much more distinctive are the country's two Muslim minorities, the Turks and the Pomaks, who account for eight per cent of the population. The Pomaks are Slavs who converted to Islam when Bulgaria was a part of the Ottoman Empire between 1396 and 1878.

The Muslims live mostly in the south, in the Rhodope Mountains which line the border with Greece. Long before they arrived, legend has it, the Rhodopes were the land of Orpheus, the poet and musician of Greek mythology. The scenery is certainly 'lyrical', a pastoral landscape of gently rising forested heights and rich mountain pastures. To the west rise the harsher, more dramatic Pirin and Rila ranges where the peaks are permanently snowcapped and where icy, glacial lakes have formed in valleys lying more than 6500 feet above sea level.

Farther north, striking from west to east across the centre of the country, are the Balkan Mountains (*balkan*

means 'mountain' in Turkish). They are known to Bulgarians as Stara Planina, 'Old Mountain'. The range has a special place in Bulgarian history as the nation's traditional heartland. From here, during and after the 7th century AD, Bulgar khans and kings established a powerful independent realm that eventually spread as far as the northern borders of the Byzantine Empire. Centuries later, when Bulgaria had fallen to the Turks, the Balkan range was the centre of Slav resistance – a mountain stronghold from which to harry the occupiers.

Some of Bulgaria's most fertile lands lie between the Balkan and Rhodope ranges. Tucked into the southern flanks of the Balkans is the Valley of the Roses, not as beautiful as it sounds, except in May when the roses flower. Roses are grown here commercially. About 70 per cent of the world's production of roses comes from the region. The Plain of Thrace spreads

A white headscarf wrapped oriental-fashion round her face protects this woman's head from the summer sun. This is simple everyday wear, distinct from the bright-coloured headdresses worn for special occasions.

Bulgaria has some of the richest traditional music in Eastern Europe. At a wedding feast in Balchik north of Varna on the Black Sea coast, a musician gets ready to strike up a tune on the gadulka. His fellows will accompany him on the tambur (drums) and accordion.

beyond the Valley of the Roses to the south. Even in the days of Homer, Thrace was known as a 'land of fertility, of thick-fleeced sheep and chargers swifter than the wind'. The soil is rich and there is plenty of water for irrigation from the River Maritsa. Vineyards, rice paddies, orchards and cotton, tobacco and vegetable fields abound, their products exported throughout Europe and the Middle East.

A huge limestone plateau – known as the Danubian Plateau – extends north from the Balkan Mountains to the Danube and the Romanian border. It is dotted with forests and large once state-owned farms. In the east, this falls away to the Dobrudzha region, including the Danube delta and the Black Sea. The Dobrudzha is Bulgaria's richest wheat-growing area. Its erstwhile smallholdings gave way to large collective farms.

Plovdiv – jewel of Thrace

Bulgaria's second-largest city, now called Plovdiv, lies on the banks of the Maritsa in the Plain of Thrace. In the old part of the city, yellow, brown and red are the dominant colours. Overhanging upper storeys lean towards the centre of streets built narrow in an effort to cut out the worst of the stifling midday heat in summer. The central gutter that runs down each street is green with moss and tufts of grass, as long as they are not washed away by one of the area's many thunderstorms. Higher up, creepers trail patterns of foliage across the brown walls of the houses and clamber up the grilles of first-floor windows.

In one shady, well-watered garden stands the house built for a rich Turkish merchant, Argir

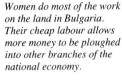

Women do most of the work on the land in Bulgaria. Their cheap labour allows more money to be ploughed into other branches of the national economy.

Kouyoumdjioglou, in the middle of the last century. Kouyoumdjioglou and his architect set out to combine the most attractive features of local architectural traditions – overhanging upper floors, the curved line of the roofs and the symmetry of the different parts of the building. They also added a few touches of their own – walls painted a delicate, pastel blue and richly ornamented with tiles and arabesques. Inside, frescoes and carved wooden ceilings demonstrate the sophistication of Bulgaria's 19th-century artists.

An appealing silence hangs over the streets of old Plovdiv, which exhibits a wealth of attractive details – a flight of old, stone moss-covered, steps here, a wooden balcony there. The cob (clay, gravel and straw) walls of even the poorest homes are often colour-washed, and most have geometric patterns inscribed round the corners of the building.

When you walk down Plovdiv's steep streets from the old town towards the Maritsa and cross the river, you find yourself in a different world. All around rise the high, white, prefabricated blocks of the new town's state-owned apartment blocks and administrative offices. Areas like this border all Bulgarian (and other socialist-bloc) cities, they are essentially the product of the Stalinist cult of industrialisation.

The countryside transformed

The huge state farms, which the post-Communist authorities have not so far dismantled, form 'agro-industrial' complexes. But the authorities have chosen not to mechanise every aspect of farming, and consequently the Bulgarian countryside still presents picturesque scenes of rural life: teams of workers weeding fields of young potatoes, lettuce or leeks; the gathering of the tomato or sweet pepper crop; the tobacco harvest.

Once the crops have been picked, they are dispatched to a plant on the farm complex for mechanical sorting.

With the need for hard currency always in mind, the best produce is sent for export to Western Europe or the Middle East, and the rest sold directly to the local market or sent to a canning factory, often also part of the complex. Similar priorities operate in Bulgaria's wine industry – the country's outstanding agricultural success story. Until the Second World War, any wines

In Bulgaria agriculture was, till the beginning of the 1980s, one of the success stories of the Communist years. It was organised on an industrial scale, and products such as capsicums and aubergines were widely exported to Western Europe. Even so, when the old regime fell in 1989 the country was virtually bankrupt.

The dustbin-like containers of steaming stew hold lunch for the women farm workers taking their midday break by the side of a field. The whole of their workday existence is organised by the cooperative.

the country produced were purely for local consumption, but now Bulgaria is the world's fifth-largest wine-exporting nation; the quality of many of its wines is highly praised by connoisseurs.

New practices have undoubtedly brought many benefits. The peasants of the Plain of Thrace, in particular, are assured of a comfortable standard of living. The primitive roads – described by the French 19th-century poet Lamartine as hopelessly muddy in winter and throwing up suffocating clouds of dust in summer – have given way to well-tarmacked roads; houses built of wattle and daub have mostly been replaced by brick houses set in trim gardens, and built with the help of state loans. Often, completion is spread out over several years, so that outside walls may be left unrendered and terraces and fences unbuilt. Inside, however, all is comfortable.

A hard-headed people

The historian Joseph Rothschild maintained: 'The Bulgarians are, on balance, rather impressively utilitarian and hard-headed, with little of the romanticism or mysticism of other Slav peoples.' Their liveliness of mind has undoubtedly helped the Bulgarians to adapt to the changes that have taken place in their country since the Second World War. On the international level, Bulgaria before the 1989 changes in Eastern Europe was known for its close – some called it, craven – allegiance to Moscow. In fact, the story was more complicated than that. Culturally, both countries have much in common: both belong to the Eastern Church; both use the Cyrillic alphabet. In the 19th century, Tsarist Russia was, for her own reasons, the most reliable supporter of the Bulgarian national movement. When in 1876 the Turks stamped out a

national uprising by massacring 29,000 Bulgarians, Russia was foremost in expressing Europe-wide indignation at what came to be known as the 'Bulgarian atrocities'. Over the next two years, Russian troops were sent to fight, in support of the Tsar's imperial expansionist policy, alongside Bulgarian 'nationalists' in the War of Liberation that led to the formation of the modern Bulgarian state.

The close ties between Bulgaria's Communist rulers and those of the former Soviet Union were, therefore, to some extent understandable, however much they incited ever stronger anti-Soviet feeling among Bulgarian intellectuals. They also brought distinct advantages. In Soviet eyes the Bulgarians' loyal and unwaveringly pro-Soviet stance made them more reliable, so less subject to interference than other satellite states. The Party in Sofia was able to pursue a more independent economic line than many of its allies. In the shareout of duties among the states of the Soviet Bloc, Bulgaria was made the 'vegetable basket' of the East – hence the large-scale investment in agriculture. But Bulgaria was also able to build up an effective industrial base that included coal mining and metal ore processing, and textiles. The result was an important change in the balance of Bulgarian society: some 60 per cent of Bulgarians now live in towns as opposed to just 20 per cent in 1946.

The Communist regime also had decidedly unpleasant sides. Its secret services, for example, showed gruesome ingenuity in disposing of the London-based, formerly high-level Communist journalist, dissident Georgi Markov in 1983, who knew too much about Zhivkov and his cronies, by pricking him with a poison-tipped umbrella. At the same time, the authorities were carrying out an 'assimilation' campaign at home against the Turks of the south.

In the mid-1980s this campaign – apparently aimed at arousing popular antagonism against the Turks to divert people's attention from a deteriorating economic situation – took the form of forcing the Turks to change their Turkish to Bulgarian names. Most mosques were closed 'for restoration' and in some areas, the use of the Turkish language, and even traditional Turkish dress, was forbidden in public places. Turks who resisted these measures were arrested, and many were shot or 'disappeared'.

In the summer of 1989, as the cracks were beginning to show in Communist regimes throughout Eastern Europe, the Party leader Todor Zhivkov ordered an intensification of the campaign. The Turks rioted and several died at the hands of the police. There was an international outcry not dissimilar to that which greeted the 'Bulgarian atrocities' just over 100 years earlier, and Zhivkov was forced to back down. He granted the Turks passports, allowing them to cross the frontier into Turkey. Thousands did so, in one of the largest mass migrations in modern European history. As a result, Bulgaria lost many of its hardest-working farmers.

Zhivkov did not survive this episode for long. His 35-year rule ended in November 1989 when he was toppled by reform-minded Communist colleagues. Since then Bulgaria has faced the usual problems of adapting to new conditions, made worse by the particularly high foreign debt inherited from the previous regime.

Sofia's National Theatre is a fine specimen of the capital's Germanic, turn-of-the-century architecture. Fountains, open-air cafés and imposing boulevards make for a pleasant, if in places rather overblown, setting.

Mountain traditions

Governments may come and go in Sofia, but in the countryside – to which most Bulgarians are still deeply attached despite the shift to the cities over the last 40 years – the struggle to earn a living has to go on. This is particularly true of the mountain areas, where farming was comparatively unaffected by the Communist reorganisation of agriculture. Farming in the mountains has always been a more precarious affair than farming on the plains, so the people have always had to supplement their living in other ways.

One of these ways has been by weaving the gloriously coloured fabrics that are still a particular speciality of the Rhodope Mountains. These fabrics, usually woven by the women, have traditionally been dominated by shades of yellow and orange, but nowadays pink designs on a white background seem to be more popular, generally simple stripes or checks, but sometimes patterns involving stylised flowers or foliage. The fabrics are used as wall hangings, table cloths, counterpanes or cushion covers.

Similar textiles are an essential part of the traditional costumes worn by Bulgarian men and women. These vary from region to region and from person to person, just about the only common factor being a long, light-coloured blouse with wide embroidered sleeves. Over this a woman may wear an elaborately braided heavy, black, sleeveless dress held in at the waist with a broad belt, or a short-sleeved frilly jacket.

Weddings are as elaborate as the costumes, and draw on various traditions of which many emphasise Bulgaria's links with the Levant. The rites start weeks or even months before the wedding itself. One of the first steps is for the groom's brother to visit the bride's father in fulfilment of an age-old ritual simulating the purchase of the young woman by her future husband's family. She later visits her betrothed's mother, and before entering the house – her future home – she traces a cross on the outside wall with honey, a symbol of fertility, but also spirituality. Inside, her future mother-in-law presents her with a white distaff (symbol of purity) and some bread and water.

Music at the wedding feast is provided by a band playing the *gayda* (bagpipes) or the *gadulka* (a stringed instrument rather like the lute) and drums. The dances include highly acrobatic, all-male performances typical of more easterly Slav countries, as well as the extremely popular (and for outsiders bafflingly complicated) *khoro*, a form of round dance.

Guardians of the nation's soul

The Orthodox Church has long had a central place in the nation's life. During the five centuries of Ottoman rule, the Orthodox monasteries – most of them situated high in the various mountain ranges – did most to keep Bulgaria's nationhood alive. Towards the end of the occupation, in the 18th and 19th centuries, they also provided Bulgaria's best schools. One such monastery is Dryanovo, not far from the medieval capital of Veliko Tarnovo in the northern foothills of the Balkan Mountains. In the 1876 uprising, a few hundred nationalists led by the schoolteacher Bacho Kiro and the monk Hariton held out there for nearly a week against 10,000 Turkish troops. The monastery still houses the rebel leader's remains and has become a national shrine. Farther south, the monastery of Troyan has a similar reputation. Here, the nationalist leader Vasil Levski, sometimes known as the 'apostle of Bulgarian freedom', often took refuge. He knew he was safe among its monks, many of whom were themselves members of revolutionary organisations.

Over the centuries the monasteries suffered a good deal at the hands of the Ottoman armies and also bands of local bandits, or *hayduks*. As a result many had to be rebuilt in the 19th century, during the Bulgarian National Revival. The building style chosen for most was the one that inspired many secular buildings, such as the Kiuyoumdjiogliu House in Plovdiv. Characteristic features included wide verandahs, projecting upper-floor windows, elaborately carved woodwork and richly coloured frescoes. Rila Monastery, in the Rila Mountains, one of Bulgaria's most popular tourist attractions, is perhaps the most outstanding example of

Rila Monastery's frescoes stand out even in comparison with Bulgaria's other monasteries. The monasteries played a key part in Bulgarian history as focal points for local resistance to Ottoman domination.

In Bulgaria, a land famous for its roses, rhododendrons grow wild in the mountains. Parks and gardens have displays of scarlet, purple and pink rhododendrons in summer.

this style. Some of its marvellous frescoes depicting rural and religious scenes, were done by Zahari Zograf, the most famous of the 19th-century muralists.

The monasteries continue to be a source of Bulgarian pride as well as religious inspiration. Even for the foreign visitor there is something inspiring about them, an impression no doubt enhanced by their usually spectacular mountain settings.

Fishermen and artists on the Black Sea coast

The Bulgarians have never been a noted maritime people, but they do have 250 miles of attractive Black Sea coastline studded with several ancient fishing ports. Many of these – for example, Sozopol – are popular with artists. Houses with stone-built ground floors and

A hooked bill and a blood-red eye give the rare lammergeier *(or bearded vulture) a ferocious aspect when seen close to. It is sometimes seen in Bulgaria's remote mountain regions, mostly from afar, as it wheels on wings some nine or ten feet wide searching the mountain ledges for carrion.*

overhanging, wooden upper storeys line mazes of picturesque streets, and, looking up, you see strings of fish hanging out to dry in the shelter of the wide eaves.

Nesebar, north-east of the one major industrial port of Burgas Clirgos, is in a particularly dramatic setting on a narrow spit of land. On a sunny day the low, blue-and-white fishermen's cottages at the tip of the peninsula stand out with particular intensity. Nesebar is also famous for its many Byzantine churches.

A few miles north of Nesebar there is a string of popular tourist resorts: Slanchev Bryag ('Sunny Beach' – the English name even some locals know it by), Zlatni Pyasatsi ('Golden Sands') and Albena. They are the Bulgarian equivalents of Spanish resorts such as Benidorm and Torremolinos, and draw hundreds of thousands of visitors every summer.

These resorts have become a showplace for traditional Bulgarian arts, crafts and cuisine – though, as always in such places, the traditions have been shorn of most of their rougher edges. Groups of musicians, often Gypsies, entertain the diners at restaurants with folk melodies. The restaurants themselves offer Levantine dishes such as *tarator* (*tsatsiki*), kebabs, stuffed vine leaves, *güvetch* (vegetable stew) and stuffed peppers.

Bulgaria is a country rich in tradition adapting itself out of necessity to the commercial demands of the modern world. Former shepherds work on farms run on an industrial scale; former peasants work in the factories of city suburbs. This neglected corner of the Balkans, whose national spirit managed to survive 500 years of Ottoman domination, is now facing the challenge of economic survival in post-socialist Europe.

The old Greek city of Nesebar, perched on a rocky cape on the Black Sea, is one of Bulgaria's major tourist attractions. Fortunately, its popularity has not destroyed the calm of its squares and narrow streets, where the houses have upper storeys of wood perched on ground floors of stone. There are numerous Byzantine churches.

Gazetteer

Commonwealth of Independent States

The Commonwealth of Independent States (CIS) was established in 1992 in the wake of the disintegration of the Soviet Union. While the CIS moves away from totalitarianism towards democracy and a capitalist economy, poverty and ethnic rivalries, which were suppressed for more than seventy years under the Communist regime, are already threatening the stability of the Commonwealth.

Earliest inhabitants
The peopling of Russia was a slow process, lasting thousands of years. Dominant among the many tribes who roamed the steppes were the Scythians (c. 500 BC), and the Sarmatians who followed two centuries later. By AD 400, Eastern Slavs from the area of modern Romania had begun farming the land between the Rivers Dnieper and Dniester, and by the 8th century their territory had increased, forming tribal regions that developed into principalities such as Kiev.

First Russian state
Kiev Russia was the first Russian state. By the early 900s the state had developed cultural and commercial links with Byzantium, and in 988 its ruler was converted to the Orthodox branch of Christianity.

As the Kiev state expanded northwards, non-Slavs came under its rule. The power of its central government weakened and by c. 1100 the state had developed into a loose union of principalities, one of which was the city of Novgorod, near the Baltic Sea. In the late 12th century Novgorod was an important trading centre, and unique among early Russian states in that the well-to-do were allowed to elect their own representatives.

Mongol invasions: 1223, 1237-40
The development of Kiev Russia was cut short in the mid-13th century by an invasion of Mongols from the east, led by the heirs of Genghis Khan. The Mongol conquest was followed by the setting up of the 'Golden Horde', a Muslim state. The Golden Horde allowed the Orthodox Church to manage its own affairs, and protected the Russian princes, provided that they paid tribute.

The rise of Moscow: 1300-1500
Rivalry developed between the princes of the different Russian territories. The church supported the princes of Moscow, the city founded in 1147 near the headwaters of the Dvina, Dnieper and Volga rivers. Its princes built up their power on the Byzantine doctrine of autocracy, combined with the ruthless methods of Tatar government. Under Muscovite rule the democratic institutions of Novgorod were suppressed.

By the end of the 15th century the ruling prince of Moscow, Ivan III (1462-1505), who saw himself as the heir to Byzantium's traditions, felt strong enough to reject the authority of the Khans (rulers) of the Golden Horde.

The religious advisers of Ivan's successors assured them that Moscow was the heir to Constantinople, the Third Rome, and 'a fourth there shall not be'.

Ivan the Terrible, the first tsar: 1533-84
Ivan IV, known as 'the Terrible', also believed in Moscow's imperial destiny. He took the title of tsar (derived from the Latin caesar*). Ivan's appetite for power and territory was insatiable, and by 1555 he had brought the whole Volga valley under his rule.*

Ivan strengthened the central government and created a ruthless security police force, to which he transferred large parts of his realm. He also created a nobility to carry out his policies. They kept their rank as long as they served him faithfully. There were still some ancient and very rich aristocratic families – the 'boyars' – but these too were brought more and more under the tsar's control. The boyars did not demand legal institutions to guarantee their status; the idea of law, with its clearly defined rights and duties, was alien to the Russian mind, and long remained so. Power and responsibility belonged to the tsar alone.

In return for their obedience, the nobility were given land and were entitled to the services of the peasants who lived on it. Serfdom was fully established in Russia by a law of 1649; by then it had virtually disappeared from most of Western Europe.

'Time of Troubles': 1598-1613
In 1598 a boyar named Boris Godunov, who had been a favourite of Ivan the Terrible, seized the throne. After Boris's death in 1605 various pretenders fought for power, with foreign support. During part of this period, known as the 'Time of Troubles', Moscow was occupied by Polish troops, and Swedish armies invaded the north. The country was ravaged by peasant rebellions, which were ruthlessly suppressed.

Peter the Great looks to Europe
The history of the modern Russian state begins with Peter I, known as 'the Great' (1682-1725). Peter believed that to become a great power, Russia had to copy modern European methods of warfare and government. He set himself to reform the country: young Russians were sent to the West to learn military and naval techniques, ship-building and industrial skills, as Peter himself had done. Foreigners were imported to reorganise the government service, and European methods of education and science were introduced. Peter rebuilt the fleet and created a new army. Russia annexed a large part of the Baltic coast, and a new capital, St Petersburg, was built on the Gulf of Finland. The city became known as 'Russia's window on to Europe', and Peter himself took the title of Emperor of Russia.

'Westernisation' and expansion
Catherine the Great (1762-96) came to the throne after the murder of her husband, Peter III. She embraced Peter the Great's work of modernisation, and advances were made in provincial administration and education.

The Russian army created by Peter the Great had become one of the most formidable in Europe. During Catherine's reign vast new territories were added to the empire by annexation and conquest. Three partitions of Poland brought millions of Ukrainians, Byelorussians, Lithuanians and Poles under Russian rule. Russia's Baltic coastline was increased. In the south, the Crimean peninsula was taken from the Ottoman Empire. Further gains were made in the Caucasus and in the steppes lying between Siberia and Turkestan.

During the 18th century, the social and political ideas of the European Enlightenment began to reach Russia. At first these were encouraged by Catherine, who entertained such men as the French philosopher Diderot at her court. But later, disturbed by the violence of the French Revolution, she began to persecute those who held liberal ideas.

Pugachev's rebellion: 1773-5
Under Catherine, industry progressed, especially in the Urals. But agriculture remained stagnant, and the poverty of the serfs grew worse. In 1773-5 a large-scale rebellion broke out in the

1 TAJIKISTAN
2 AZERBAIJAN
3 LITHUANIA
4 ARMENIA

Urals and Volga regions, led by Emilian Pugachev. Catherine crushed the rebellion and Pugachev was executed in Moscow.

Catherine's grandson, Alexander I, planned to reform the empire. While retaining a centralised state he wanted to ensure that it worked efficiently and that as its absolute ruler he would be a benefactor of the people. His plans were frustrated by war with France.

Napoleon invades: 1812
Napoleon led 675,000 men into Russia in a bid to crush his last major rival on the European continent. At the Battle of Borodino, outside Moscow, both sides took heavy losses. The Russians retreated and the French entered Moscow. But the tsar rejected offers of peace, and Napoleon, fearing his army's food supplies would not outlast the Russian winter, decided to retreat into Poland. Illness, hunger and the extreme cold of the Russian winter reduced the French army to a fighting force of only 30,000 men.

Triumph of conservatism: 1815
Russia's victories over Napoleon strengthened the hand of the extreme conservatives. Liberal Russians wished to change the

regime but they were unsuccessful and a revolt in December 1825 was quickly crushed.

Under Nicholas I (1825-55), autocracy was upheld without the least concession to current liberal thought. The tsar felt called upon to defend monarchical government even outside Russia's boundaries: in 1848, Russian forces suppressed revolution in Romania, and in 1849 they helped the Habsburgs of Austria to crush the Hungarians. These actions gained Nicholas the label of 'gendarme of Europe'.

War in the Crimea: 1854-6
Soon Nicholas became involved in war in the Crimea, which was largely brought about by British and French determination to check Russian designs on Turkey. Russia was defeated: the campaign revealing the inefficiency of the army commanders, the weakness of its supply services and communications and the inability of Russia's economy to support a major war.

The 'Tsar Liberator'
Alexander II, who came to the throne in 1855, was determined to reform, modernise and strengthen Russia. He believed that reform should be the work of a benevolent sovereign, operating

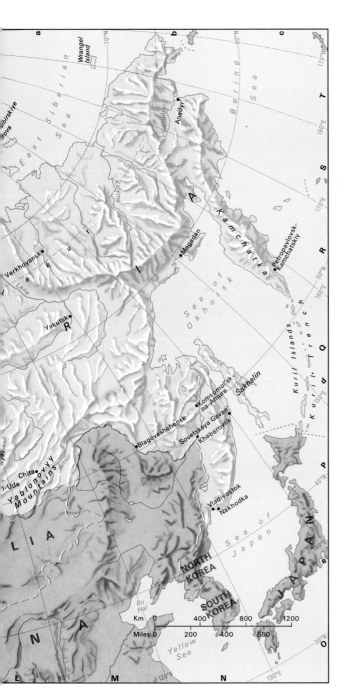

Industrial revolution reaches Russia
Under the despotic rule of Alexander III and that of his successor, Nicholas II (1894-1917), Russia went through the decisive early stages of an industrial revolution. The price of industrial expansion was paid by the peasants, whose taxes were spent on industry and the army. Government neglect of agriculture, and the problem of over-population, were the main causes of growing peasant poverty.

National oppression: *c.* 1890
Russia was a multinational empire, with less than half of its population Russian. In the 1890s the government embarked on a new policy of 'Russification' whereby all subjects were ordered to consider themselves part of the Russian nation and to adopt the Russian language and the Orthodox religion. This policy made enemies of peoples who until then had been loyal to the regime. Special forms of oppression were reserved for the Jews. They endured many legal forms of discrimination, and also had to face frequent mob attacks (pogroms) on their lives and property. These outrages, carried out by gangs of poor townspeople, were tolerated by the police; there were often fatalities.

Russo-Japanese war: 1904-5
A policy of territorial and economic expansion in the Far East brought conflict with Japan. Japan surprised the world by defeating the Russian army, and annihilating the tsar's fleet in the Tsushima Straits. Humiliation in war brought political unrest in Russia to boiling point.

While still trying to stave off defeat by Japan, Russia was shaken by large-scale revolt at home, the Revolution of 1905. It was sparked off by the events of 'Bloody Sunday' on January 22, when demonstrators marching to petition the tsar in the Winter Palace in St Petersburg were shot down by the troops. By the end of the month nearly half a million workers were on strike; in some cities there was street fighting, peasants rose against their landlords in provinces all over Russia, and workers in St Petersburg armament factories set up the first soviets (workers' councils). Units of the armed forces revolted; mutiny occurred on the Potemkin, *a battleship of the Black Sea fleet. In October a national railway strike brought the regime to the verge of collapse, and the tsar, Nicholas II, was compelled to introduce a constitution.*

Parliamentary experiment: 1905-7
The constitution established a Duma (parliament); but though it was elected on a broad franchise, it had little real power to bring about reform. In 1907 the newly appointed prime minister, Peter Stolypin, reduced the franchise. Subsequent Dumas had conservative majorities, but even they were antagonised by the authoritarian behaviour of ministers and officials. The imperial government, under Stolypin, made efforts to reform Russia, notably in education and agriculture. Industry also advanced rapidly. But after Stolypin's assassination in 1911, the tsarist regime reverted to its former reactionary character.

Russia in the First World War: 1914-17
Russia's armies suffered appalling casualties and defeats in the First World War. A majority in the Duma became hostile to the government, largely because even the best conservative ministers were replaced by inferior politicians – due, it was claimed, to the influence of a Georgian monk, Rasputin, on the easily led tsar and tsarina. Poor administration caused the disruption of agriculture, war industries and transport.

'February Revolution': 1917
In 1917, strikes and demonstrations against the government escalated as workers in the capital took to the streets. Mutinies occurred in army units. Troops joined forces with demonstrators, and the imperial regime ceased to function. Nicholas II abdicated and a newly formed provincial government proclaimed Russia a republic.

through a strong bureaucracy, though discounting public opinion and private initiative. In 1861 serfdom was abolished and the peasants were enabled to buy land, paying annuities to the government which in turn compensated the landowners. In practice, the landlords' control of the serfs was replaced by that of government officials. In 1864 a modern judicial system was set up, and citizens in the provinces were allowed to take part in local government. The tsar refused, however, to institute any central parliament.

Assassination of Alexander II: 1881
Alexander's government had tried to make valuable reforms, but these did not satisfy the political extremists. Young educated Russians were appalled by the gap between the material progress of the West and the backwardness of Russia; and between the comparatively enlightened administration of European countries and the corruption, brutality and unpredictability of Russian government. Revolution seemed the only remedy and in 1881 a revolutionary group, the 'People's Will', assassinated the tsar. His successor, Alexander III (1881-94), was a staunch autocrat and all plans for reform were shelved.

These events took place in March but are known as 'the February Revolution', because of a difference of 13 days between the calendar then used in Russia and that used in the rest of Europe. The February Revolution initiated the Russian Revolution, which lasted more than three years and fell into three main stages: the struggle of the moderates to hold power, the Bolshevik 'October Revolution', and the long period of civil war which followed.

In the first eight months of the Revolution, the moderate socialist politicians of the Duma, led by Alexander Kerensky, struggled to establish themselves in power. Their failure to do so was due to the breakdown of the machinery of government, the appeal to the masses by the extreme left and the hostility of conservatives and army commanders. The moderates' fate was sealed by their failure to beat the Germans or to extricate Russia from the war.

'October Revolution': 1917
On November 7, the extreme left-wing Communist group known as the Bolsheviks seized power. Their leader was Vladimir Ilyich Lenin, a theorist and practitioner of revolution, who had built up the party since 1903 according to his own ideas of revolutionary organisation and tactics. This revolution was almost bloodless. The military action was planned and led by Leon Trotsky, a former opponent of Lenin who had now become his closest comrade-in-arms.

Civil war: 1918-20
The Bolsheviks soon established a monopoly of political power. But in 1918 civil war broke out. Bolshevik forces were opposed at various times by democrats, military dictators and by nationalist movements among the non-Russian peoples. From the beginning of 1919 the anti-Communists or White Russians received large supplies of war material, as well as military advice, from the Allied powers of the West. The war brought massive bloodshed, destruction and starvation. Both sides tortured and executed opponents and robbed peasants of their crops. The end of 1920 saw a Communist victory, but Russia was exhausted.

Establishment of the USSR: 1920-2
The new rulers of Russia set up a rigid system of government which was supposedly based on the soviets (workers' councils). In practice, power was concentrated first in the hands of the central committee of the Communist Party and then in those of the Politburo, which decided all major policy questions, and the Secretariat, which was responsible for appointments within the party. The new government promised freedom to the non-Russian nationalities; but despite the establishment of 'republics' Moscow still kept absolute control.

Stalin wins struggle for power: 1924-9
After Lenin's death in 1924, a struggle for the succession developed. Within three years this was won by the party secretary, Joseph Stalin, due to his control over the appointment of party officials, his pursuit of moderate economic policies, and his appeal to Russian national pride. He maintained that Russian workers and peasants could, by their own efforts, 'build socialism in one country'. His rivals argued that the Revolution's success could be maintained only if it spread throughout the world, or at least to such advanced industrial countries as Britain, Germany and the United States. Its failure to do so weakened the position of Stalin's arch rival Trotsky and his supporters. Trotsky, exiled in 1928, was murdered in Mexico in 1940, reputedly by a Stalinist agent.

Drive for industrialisation: 1928-37
Once firmly in control, Stalin changed his moderate economic policy. He was convinced that Russia was in great danger until it became a full-scale industrial power, and he determined to achieve this at any cost. The result was the forced 'collectivisation' of agriculture and a drive for intensive

industrialisation in the first two Five-Year Plans (1928-37). The effect of collectivisation was not so much to make farming more efficient as to ensure that a much larger share of the crops was taken by the state, at very low prices. The peasants paid the bill for industrialisation.

Forced collectivisation caused immense upheaval, leading to the starvation of millions of peasants and the destruction of over half of Russia's livestock. Of those peasants who survived, many millions were herded into the new industrial and mining centres and construction sites.

Mass suffering produced discontent, which took political form in agitation against the regime, especially among the non-Russian peoples. Stalin's response was to give the security police almost unlimited power and to pursue 'Russification' as ruthlessly as the tsars had done. Millions were deported to forced labour camps; factories and farms were set up in remote parts of the country, under control of the security police.

Purge of the party: 1936-9
By the mid-1930s Stalin's attention had turned to the removal of real or possible enemies inside the Communist Party. In the 'Great Purge' of 1936-9, the existing leaders of the party, the central ministries, industry and the armed forces were swept away. The purges started as an attack on the surviving followers of Stalin's former rivals, but the number of arrests got out of control as police officials competed with each other in unmasking 'enemies of the people'. Every level of society was hit. Especially sensational were the 'show trials' of leading figures, and the execution of army commanders in 1937. About half the officer corps, from the rank of major upwards, were arrested. Stalin called a halt to the purges in 1939.

Second World War: 1941-5
The Russians believed that if the victors and vanquished of 1918 were reconciled, the Soviet Union would be in danger of attack from a united capitalist world. Thus they supported Germany against the West in the 1920s and the West against Germany from 1935 to 1939. They turned to Germany once more from 1939 to 1941. In 1941, however, the Russians found themselves faced with the full might of the German war machine.

Hitler's invasion in 1941 was the first major test of Soviet Russia's strength. At first the Germans achieved great success, but with the heroic Russian defence of Stalingrad (now Volgograd) the tide turned. By 1945 the Soviet Union's armies had advanced from the depths of Russia to control more than half of Europe.

'Cult of Personality': 1945-53
Just as the defeat of Napoleon in 1815 had strengthened tsarist conservatism, so the victory of 1945 increased the prestige of Stalin and his regime. In the following years a totalitarian autocracy prevailed in Russia; Stalin was glorified by a 'cult of personality', which accorded him a god-like status. Party, army, bureaucracy and security police were tools in his hands, and he manipulated each according to his whim.

The alliance between the Soviet Union, Britain and the United States broke down at this time and gave place to the 'Cold War'. The determination of Russia to impose its political system on Eastern Europe, by force if necessary, alarmed Western opinion. Deadlock was reached over the future of Germany. In 1948, the Soviet Army tried to blockade Berlin, but the West kept the city supplied by an airlift. In 1949 NATO was set up and the United States was committed to defend Western Europe against a Soviet attack.

'Thaw' after Stalin
When Stalin died in March 1953, his successors, distrusting each other, established what they called 'collective leadership'. The feared and hated chief of the MVD (security police), Lavrenti Beria, Stalin's closest confidant, was arrested and executed. After his death the powers of the security police were

curtailed, many political prisoners were released, there was some intellectual liberalisation, and the Russian people received more and better consumer goods.

By 1957 one man, Nikita Krushchev, had emerged as the leader of the Soviet Union. He avoided the excesses of Stalin's 'personality cult'. He himself denounced this cult, the police terror and 'show trials', in a historic speech in 1956 at the Party congress. Krushchev made enemies among the leadership of the party; in particular he offended the leaders of the armed forces by cutting the defence budget to pay for more consumer goods. In 1964 he was voted out of power by the party's Central Committee. He was succeeded by Leonid Brezhnev as Party First Secretary and Alexei Kosygin as Prime Minister. The new leadership continued Krushchev's policy of trying to achieve 'peaceful co-existence' with the West, but at the same time the country's armed forces were strengthened.

Rebellious satellites
After Stalin's death, Russia's control of its satellites in Eastern Europe was somewhat relaxed. This led to outbursts of national feeling, culminating in the Hungarian Revolution of October 1956. The Soviet rulers suppressed the revolt by armed invasion. In 1968, a new crisis occurred in Czechoslovakia, where the leader, Alexander Dubcek, led a movement to reform the political system. This too was suppressed by the Russian army, which moved into the country in massive strength. Dubcek was soon replaced by a compliant pro-Soviet leadership.

Cuba missile crisis: 1962
While maintaining a stranglehold over half of Europe, the Soviet rulers after Stalin did their best to exploit anti-European and anti-American feeling in Asia, Africa and Latin America. Fidel Castro's Cuba became a centre of Soviet influence. Krushchev's attempt to set up a nuclear missile base there in 1962 brought the world to the brink of nuclear war. He was forced to withdraw the missiles after a confrontation with the US president, John F. Kennedy.

Quarrel with Communist China
In the Far East, the victory of the Chinese Communists in the civil war in 1949 seemed likely to strengthen Soviet power in the world. But during the 1960s animosity developed between the two countries. In 1969, their armed forces clashed along the frontier on the River Amur. The Chinese accused the Russians of betraying the principles of Marxist-Leninism; the Russians replied by bitterly accusing China of copying all the worst features of Stalinism, especially the 'personality cult'.

A superpower shares world dominance
At the beginning of the 1970s Soviet Russia was a superpower, with the full panoply of nuclear arms and intercontinental missiles, but it faced two formidable rivals – the United States, a still more powerful superpower, and China, potentially a third. The advance of post-war Soviet technology had been highlighted by the launching of the world's first artificial space satellite – Sputnik I – in 1959 and the first manned spaceship in 1961.

Détente
The three world powers jockeyed for position, brandishing political and economic weapons and negotiating with sanctions, embargoes, aid to Third World nations and cultural sabotage. Increased Soviet presence in Asia, especially in Vietnam after 1975, was countered by accords between China, Japan and the USA. A period of détente between Russia and the USA came to an end when the USSR invaded Afghanistan. The crisis in Poland between 1978 and 1983, when the Solidarity movement challenged Poland's Marxist government, provoked Soviet pressure on Poland, and was seen as the USSR's determination to preserve its hegemony in Eastern Europe. Brezhnev's death in 1982 was followed by two brief periods in which the USSR was headed first by Yuri Andropov (1982-4) and then Konstantin Chernenko (1984-5). Andropov tried to institute economic reforms, but died before being able to do so, while Chernenko revived the détente with the West. It was his successor, however, Mikhail Gorbachev, who was left to normalise relations with the USA.

The end of the Soviet Union
In 1986 Gorbachev initiated a series of political and economic reforms. Relations with the West improved dramatically, Soviet troops were withdrawn from Afghanistan, political prisoners were released and a degree of political plurality was introduced.

However, the economy did not improve, and Gorbachev's popularity abroad was not reflected at home, where the food queues were lengthening. He tried to steer a middle course between the hard-line Communists and the reformers, led by Boris Yeltsin, who favoured a swift change to a capitalist-style market economy.

In August 1991 a conservative-led coup failed to oust Gorbachev. But the days of the Soviet Union were numbered. Gorbachev resigned in December 1991, opening the way for Boris Yeltsin, the President of Russia, to disband the Soviet Union and set up the Commonwealth of Independent States.

Czechoslovakia

The name of Czechoslovakia reflects the fact that the country is made up of two major nationalities – the Czechs and the Slovaks. The republic came into existence after the First World War but, after 74 years, the people have decided to divide the country into the Czech Lands and Slovakia.

Early conquerors
In the 1st century BC, the Celtic settlers of the Czech lands were conquered by Germanic tribes. By AD 500 these tribes had been displaced by nomadic Slavs, among whom were the Czechs, moving from the east. By the 7th century these Slavs had set up a group of states, which c. 800 were absorbed into Charlemagne's empire. After the break-up of the empire the Slavs formed the kingdom of Greater Moravia. But at the end of the 9th century this was destroyed by Magyar invasion. The region of Slovakia, in the east, came under Magyar rule.

Under the sway of Austria
By the late Middle Ages the Czechs had established the kingdom of Bohemia as a prosperous and well-run monarchy,

thanks to the efficient rule of several monarchs, including Charles IV, who was also a Holy Roman Emperor.

The Czechs' strong nationalist feelings were fostered by the religious teachings of Jan Hus (1369-1415), a teacher at the University of Prague. Foreshadowing Luther, he put forward the idea of a national church for Bohemia, independent of the dictates of the pope in Rome. Though Hus was burnt at the stake for heresy, his teachings continued to inspire Bohemian patriotism. However, in 1526 Bohemia fell under the sway of the Habsburg dynasty when Ferdinand of Austria succeeded to the Bohemian throne. In 1618 the Protestant Bohemian nobility, invoking the name of Jan Hus, rebelled and broke away from the Catholic Habsburgs. After the 'defenestration of Prague', in which the emperor's envoys were thrown out of a window, they elected the German Protestant Prince Frederick, the son-in-law of James I of England, as king.

Czech independence was short-lived. At the Battle of the White Mountain, outside Prague, in 1620, the Czech armies were totally defeated by those of Austria and its Roman Catholic allies; Bohemia was reduced to the status of a province of the Austrian Empire.

For almost three centuries, Bohemia remained under

CZECHOSLOVAKIA AT A GLANCE

Area	127,889 square miles
Population	15,550,000
Capital	Prague
Government	Federal republic
Currency	Koruna (crown) = 100 haler
Languages	Czech, Slovak, Hungarian
Religion	Christian (67% Roman Catholic, 10% Protestant)
Climate	Continental, with hot summers and cold winters; average temperature in Prague ranges from -4-1°C (25-34°F) in January to 14-23°C (57-73°F) in July
Main primary products	Potatoes, sugar beet, cereals, livestock; coal, lignite, iron ore, uranium, mercury, antimony, magnesium
Major industries	Iron and steel, transport equipment, machinery, cement, chemicals, fertilisers, textiles
Main exports	Machinery, motor vehicles, iron and steel, chemicals, footwear, textile yarns and fabrics, food, clothing, coal, railway vehicles
Annual income per head (US$)	4500
Population growth (per thous/yr)	3
Life expectancy (yrs) Male	70
Female	74

Austrian rule. In 1848 the intellectuals of Prague, in the first stirrings of Czech revolt, organised a congress to demand independence for Bohemia. But the revolutionaries were weak and divided; they were speedily crushed by the Austrian army.

Despite the failure of the 1848 revolution, the nationalist movement continued to grow, aided by the slow disintegration of the Austrian Empire, as its subject peoples began to agitate against Habsburg rule. The achievements of composers such as Smetana and Dvorak, and of writers such as Franz Kafka, showed the vitality of Czech culture over this long period.

Independence: 1918

Independence came with the final collapse of the Habsburg Empire in 1918. Under the leadership of Thomas Masaryk and Edvard Benes, Czechoslovakia developed into a liberal democracy, with higher standards of political tolerance and economic prosperity than many of its neighbours.

But the new country had serious racial problems. It contained a 3.5 million-strong German minority, as well as Hungarians and Ukrainian Ruthenes. Racial tensions were aggravated by the Depression of the 1930s, which also worsened the plight of the peasants.

Munich: 1938

The Germans, concentrated in the Sudetenland just inside Czechoslovakia's western border, formed the most active racial minority. The Sudeten German Party, led by Konrad Henlein and supported by Nazi Germany, demanded to join the Reich. When the Czechs made a defence agreement with the USSR in 1935, German pressure increased and Hitler threatened war if the Sudeten Germans were not given the right of 'self-determination'.

France and Britain refused to protect the Czechs, and by the Munich agreement of September 1938, persuaded Czechoslovakia to give the Sudeten territory, which included all the Czech frontier defences, to Germany.

The Munich agreement further weakened Czechoslovakia by dividing it into a federal state, with a Czech government in Prague and a Slovak government in Slovakia. In March 1939, the Prague government dismissed the Slovak government under its Catholic leader, Monsignor Tiso, who then appealed to Hitler for support. German troops were ordered to invade Prague.

From liberation to Communism: 1945-8

With the outbreak of the Second World War in September 1939, the Allies recognised a Czech government-in-exile under Benes, who had become president in 1935. Mindful of Munich,

he took especial care to keep on good terms with the USSR, signing a treaty of friendship with the Russians in 1943. In 1945 Soviet troops liberated the country and Benes returned to power.

Elections were held in 1946 in which the Communists, with 38 per cent of the vote, emerged as the strongest single party. Their leader, Klement Gottwald, formed a government which still included 12 non-Communist ministers. But in February 1948 these ministers resigned in protest at Communist infiltration of the police.

In new elections, the Communists, backed by the Soviet Union which threatened to send in the Red Army, were virtually unopposed. After the Communist takeover in 1948, the Czech patriot leader, Jan Masaryk (son of Thomas), met a violent death, perhaps by suicide; the official explanation was that he threw himself from a window. Benes died later in the year and Gottwald took over the presidency.

The new Communist regime was one of the harshest in the Soviet bloc, and for the next 20 years Czech life was marked by political purges, rigid censorship, arbitrary imprisonment and suppression of freedoms.

Soviet invasion: 1968

Hard-line leadership came to an end in 1968, when Alexander Dubcek became the new leader. He set in motion an ambitious programme of 'Socialism with a human face', designed to liberalise the regime and give the Czech people more economic and political freedom. The USSR viewed these reforms with alarm. Dubcek was summoned to Moscow and told to halt his programme. On his refusal to do so, Soviet, East German, Polish, Hungarian and Bulgarian troops and tanks invaded Czechoslovakia in August 1968.

Czechoslovakia's freedom was shortlived. In April 1969, Dubcek was forced to resign and was replaced by Russian-backed Gustav Husak. The reform programme was abandoned and Dubcek supporters were purged.

The Velvet Revolution: 1989

In November 1989, hundreds of thousands of Czechoslovaks took to the streets to protest against Husak's government. The democracy movement found charismatic leaders in Dubcek (who returned from internal exile) and Vaclav Havel, the playwright and former political prisoner. Husak finally resigned in December and Havel was elected president.

In 1992 the Czechs and Slovaks voted to go their separate ways: the country was to be divided into Slovakia and the Czech Lands.

Hungary

Before the First World War, Hungary was the partner of Austria in ruling the vast Austro-Hungarian Empire, which stretched across the greater part of central Europe.

Before the Magyars

The Middle Danube plain, on which Hungary lies, was settled by Stone Age hunters and herders more than 80,000 years ago. The plain was later occupied by Scythic peoples, followed by Celts and Slavs, and in the 1st century BC much of the west was part of the Roman province of Pannonia. Pannonia was overrun by nomadic eastern warriors – Goths, Huns and Turkic Avars – c. AD 200. The two latter groups were related to the Magyars, the main national group of Hungary.

Magyar colonisation: c. 800

In the 9th century, the Magyars defeated the tribes of the plains and set up their own dynasty which lasted until the 14th century. One of the greatest of the Magyar rulers was St Stephen. He introduced Christianity, centralised the government to reduce the powers of the Magyar chieftains and, with his successors, set up Hungary to become one of the most powerful states of central Europe and the northern Balkans. In the early 16th century, the country was threatened by the westward advance of the Ottoman Turks. In 1526, Louis II, the last king of an independent Hungary, was killed in the Battle of Mohacs, and the Turks went on to destroy much of the country.

Habsburgs take power: 1526-1711

The Habsburg rulers of Austria now fought the Turks for control of Hungary. The struggle between them lasted on and off until 1699, when all but a small part of Hungary came under Habsburg rule.

An attempt by Leopold of Austria to end the privileges of the Hungarian land-owning nobility caused them to revolt in 1704. Agreement was eventually reached in the Peace of Szatmar in 1711: the Hungarians promised to remain loyal to the Habsburgs; in return the Habsburgs accepted the Hungarian landowners' right to rule themselves.

Growing independence from Vienna: 1711-1867

In 1848, Lajos Kossuth, the Hungarian nationalist leader, led a revolution to secure greater independence for Hungary. But Russia sent an army to help Austria crush this revolt and Vienna became firmly in control of Hungary.

But after Austria was weakened by its defeat at the hands of Prussia in 1866, Emperor Franz Josef was forced to make far-reaching concessions to Hungary. An Austro-Hungarian dual monarchy was established, with an emperor common to both Austria and Hungary. Hungary itself became an equal power in the running of the empire.

Independent Hungary: 1918-45

After the collapse of the Habsburg monarchy at the end of the First World War, a Hungarian republic was proclaimed under the leadership of Count Mihaly Karolyi. Karolyi soon resigned and the Communists took power under Bela Kun. Five months later his regime was brought down by Romanian intervention.

Leading 'counter-revolutionaries' formed a government under Admiral Horthy, the commander of the Austro-Hungarian navy in the First World War, who took the title of regent. Under his regency, Hungary was dominated by a succession of right-wing governments, some of whose leaders, such as Gyula Gömbös, were open admirers of Hitler and Mussolini.

Peace with the Allies had been made by the Treaty of Trianon in 1920. Hungary was forced to cede large areas of its territory to Romania and the newly independent nations of Czechoslovakia and Yugoslavia. The recovery of these 'lost territories' became the cardinal aim of Hungarian foreign

policy between the wars, and led the government to ally itself with Hitler and Mussolini in the 1930s. Under German pressure, Hungary declared war on Russia in 1941, and its troops fought alongside the Germans on the Eastern front.

Communist takeover: 1947

With Nazi Germany facing defeat, Soviet troops occupied Hungary in the winter of 1944-5. But the Hungarian people were strongly anti-Communist, and in the elections of 1945 only a few Communist candidates were successful. However, in 1947, having secured key posts in the government, the Communists took power, with Russian backing. A new Soviet-type constitution was proclaimed in 1948. It made Hungary a one-party state, which was ruled on Stalinist lines, with full resort to police terror, by Matyas Rakosi until 1953.

Revolt and repression

After Stalin's death in 1953, Rakosi was replaced as prime minister by the more liberal Imre Nagy. Many political prisoners were released. In October 1956 a large-scale anti-Communist rising broke out in Budapest. Influenced by public demonstrations, a new government under Nagy promised to introduce a neutralist foreign policy and a multi-party democratic regime. In response, Soviet tanks and troops invaded Hungary, setting up a pro-Russian government under Janos Kadar. Nagy proclaimed Hungary's neutrality and appealed to the free world to intervene. But Soviet forces crushed the revolt, after bloody street-fighting in Budapest. Thousands of refugees fled to Austria and Nagy was arrested and eventually executed.

Cautious economic reforms

After the catastrophe of 1956, the Kadar government decided that reforms could only be introduced slowly. The reforms of the 1960s were mainly concentrated on economic policy, which was defined in the 'New Economic Mechanism' in 1968. They brought about a substantial improvement in living standards, and there was also a limited degree of political toleration. But the government was also careful not to alienate the Soviet Union by showing any public disagreement with Soviet policy.

The curtain falls

In response to Gorbachev's calls for reform in Eastern Europe, many of the conservative members of the Hungarian government were replaced in 1988. In May 1989 Hungary opened its border with Austria, allowing thousands of East Germans to escape to the West. Free multi-party elections were held in 1990 and a new government was formed by the centre-right Democratic Forum.

HUNGARY AT A GLANCE

Area 35,920 square miles

Population 10,620,000

Capital Budapest

Government Republic

Currency Forint = 100 filler

Language Magyar (Hungarian)

Religion Christian (55% Roman Catholic, 22% Protestant), Jewish (1%)

Climate Continental; average temperature in Budapest ranges from -4-1°C (25-34°F) in January to 16-28°C (61-82°F) in July

Main primary products Cereals, potatoes, sugar beet, fruit and vegetables, grapes, livestock, timber; bauxite, coal, lignite, oil and natural gas

Major industries Agriculture, iron, steel, textiles, chemicals, machinery, transport equipment, forestry, timber products, mining

Main exports Food, machinery, chemicals, motor vehicles, clothing, iron and steel

Annual income per head (US$) 1900

Population growth (per thous/yr) Declining

Life expectancy (yrs) Male 67 **Female** 75

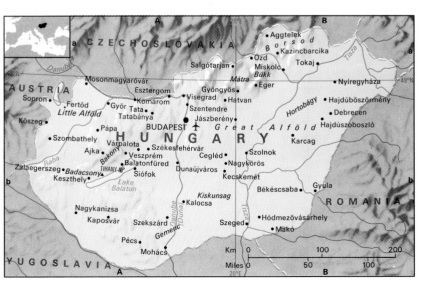

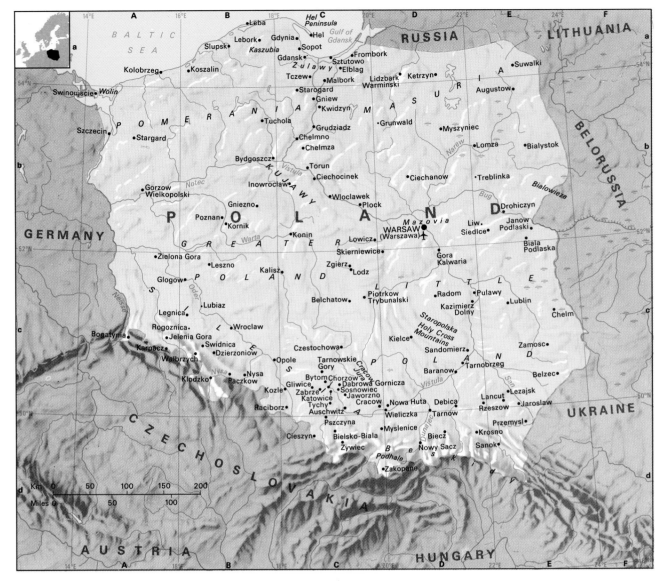

Poland

Under the great Jagiellon dynasty in the 16th century, Poland was the heart of an empire stretching across Europe from the Baltic to the Black Sea. But for much of their modern history the Poles have been a nation without a country. From 1795 to 1918 the Polish state vanished entirely from the map of Europe, victim of a series of 'partitions' carried out by its powerful and acquisitive neighbours. The Poles recovered their independence after the First World War, only to see their land dismembered again a generation later. Through all these upheavals the Poles have never lost their tradition of intense patriotism, which dates back 1000 years.

Emergence of a nation
The Polish nation was formed in the 10th century AD from a group of Slav tribes occupying the plains through which the River Vistula winds to the Baltic Sea. The name Poland came from the dominant tribe, the Polians. The Poles were converted to Christianity from 966 onwards and, fearful of invasion by pagan German tribes, accepted protection from the Holy Roman Emperor.

A powerful state was created by the next Polish ruler, Boleslaw I, who waged war against the Romans in the west and pushed his eastern boundaries as far as Kiev. This state broke up when, just over a century after Boleslaw's death, Boleslaw III left his domain divided among his sons on his death. Poland was left unable to resist the challenge of new and

powerful foreign enemies and the country was swept by Tatar invasion in 1241. In the west a new German military order, the Teutonic Knights, threatened the Poles but was destroyed.

To improve its prosperity, each small state encouraged immigration from the more advanced West; many of the immigrants were Jews escaping Christian persecution in other countries.

Revival of Poland
Poland was reunited under Wladislaw the Short (1320-33). His son, Casimir the Great, continued the revival of Poland during his long and peaceful reign, founding the University of Cracow in 1364, and improving life for the Jews and the peasants. Towards the end of the 14th century, Poland became strongly associated with Lithuania in the east when Casimir's granddaughter, Jadwiga, married Ladislaw Jagiello, Grand Duke of Lithuania. The Jagiellon dynasty which they founded ruled Poland for the next 200 years.

Jagiellon dynasty
Under the Jagiellons, Poland became one of the most powerful states in Europe with its territories stretching from the Baltic to the Black Sea. The arts and sciences flourished; it was at Cracow University that the Polish astronomer Copernicus founded modern astronomy.

However, Jagiellon Poland had two weaknesses – the old warrior nobility was kept in check but not deprived of its powers, and moreover the state was multinational with the

Poles forming the minority group. One Jagiellon ruler tried to form a Polish empire but, having merged Poland and Lithuania into one state, he died without heirs, and the Polish nobles reasserted their old-established right to elect a new ruler. After this no Polish ruler was in a position to consolidate the empire, and the decline of Poland began.

Rule by elected kings
As the nobles were too jealous to elect a king from amongst themselves, it became customary to invite foreigners in to rule Poland. Many of these foreign rulers dragged the country into war to satisfy their own non-Polish ambitions, and by the mid-17th century Poland had been exhausted by war and the squabbles of its nobility. Poland's last great military success was in 1683 when its armies lifted the Turkish siege of Vienna, thus ending the Islamic threat to Europe.

Powerful enemies – Russia to the east, and Sweden to the north – emerged to threaten Poland, and by the early 18th century the country had become a battleground for foreign armies.

Partition of Poland
Russia, having defeated Sweden, became Poland's main enemy in the 18th century, although Prussia and Austria were also hostile to their neighbour. In 1772 all three powers invaded and stripped Poland of a quarter of its territory. Tadeus Kosciuszko desperately led his countrymen against the Russians and Prussians but was defeated near Warsaw. Two years later the last king of Poland abdicated and his country vanished from the map of Europe, swallowed up in a third partition between Russia, Prussia and Austria.

Poland in bondage
For over a century Poland lived only in the hearts and minds of its people. There were unsuccessful revolts against the Russians but these were severely crushed. Prussia, too, attacked Polish patriotism by restricting the use of the Polish language and by encouraging thousands of Germans to settle in its Polish territories. Austria showed more consideration for Polish feelings.

Hope came with the outbreak of the First World War in 1914. The tsar's armies were unable to hold their Polish territory and the Germans marched into Warsaw promising Poland independence. The Poles were not taken in by these promises and refused to fight with the Germans. They looked with more hope to their allies, especially the United States. Their hopes were answered when President Wilson pledged the Allies to create a 'united, independent and autonomous Poland'. In November 1918, when Germany surrendered, the Poles disarmed the German garrison in Warsaw and proclaimed an independent republic.

Poland reborn: 1918-23
The new state faced many problems, especially over the question of frontiers, and it was not until 1923 that the last frontier was settled. The new Poland's only access to the sea was by the so-called 'Polish corridor', which cut through German territory, dividing East Prussia from the rest of Germany.

Pilsudski's Poland
Inexperienced in self-government, the liberated Poles found it difficult to create a strong democratic system. In addition there were considerable economic problems. Marshal Pilsudski seized power in a military coup in 1926, resigned in 1928, seized it again in 1930 and remained master of Poland until his death in 1935. He was succeeded by Marshal Smigly-Rydz, who headed a government dominated by a clique of army officers and landowners.

Pilsudski had aligned himself with France, forming part of an alliance designed to deal with any German resurgence. But after Hitler came to power in 1933, Poland's rulers turned towards the Nazis as they sympathised with much of Hitler's ideology. It was only after Hitler's march into Prague early in

1939 that the Polish government accepted guarantees of assistance from Britain and France in the event of German attack.

Invasion and partition: 1939
On 1 September, 1939, using as pretexts the Polish corridor and the German claim to Danzig (which had been under League of Nations control), Hitler launched on Poland the blitzkrieg which began the Second World War. Without warning, 2000 German aircraft bombed Warsaw and the Polish airfields.

After 17 days another blow struck Poland when the Red Army swept almost unopposed across the Eastern frontier. This was the result of the Nazi-Soviet Pact – a non-agression treaty agreed by Hitler and Stalin just before the outbreak of war. Its secret clauses divided Poland between the two powers in yet another partition, and the Red Army had come to take its share of territory. The Polish government fled to safety in Romania, the last defenders of Warsaw were obliterated by bombardment, and very soon Poland lay divided under the heel of its German and Russian conquerors. When the Nazi blitzkrieg struck the Soviet Union in June 1941, the Germans quickly overran the rest of Poland.

Rule by terror: 1939-45
For over five years, the Poles suffered from the unbelievable inhumanity of the Nazi rule. Over 6 million, including 3 million Jews, were exterminated by genocide. The Jews did not give in without a struggle, and the Warsaw ghetto rose. Its heroic existence ended with the massacre of all its remaining inhabitants. In August 1944, as the Russians drove the Germans back towards Warsaw, the Polish resistance seized Warsaw and held it for two months against the Germans. While the Poles were blasted into submission, Soviet forces remained inactive outside the city.

Meanwhile, the legal Polish government continued the war in exile based in London. They raised naval, military and air forces which played a leading role in the war. In July 1944, however, a rival Soviet-backed regime was set up at Lublin.

Communist Poland
The Red Army occupied Poland in 1944 and despite pledged free elections in 1947, it was soon plain to thousands of exiles returning home that there was only a chilly welcome for them in a Poland dominated by the Kremlin. Since the Second World War Poland has followed the same course as other Eastern European countries subservient to the Russians. There have been purges, persecutions and brief 'thaws'.

The Solidarity movement
Rapid economic expansion occurred during the early 1970s, but consumer prices spiralled upwards due to rising costs, growing debt and defence spending. In mid-1980 Polish workers staged massive strikes demanding wage rises, independent labour unions and political reform. The extent of the strike movement, which spread throughout Poland's social structure, brought the nation to a standstill and toppled the government. In November 1980 the government approved the charter of the Solidarity Union – the first free labour union officially recognised in a Communist state. A year later the Communist Party declared martial law and Lech Walesa, the Solidarity leader, and other activists were imprisoned. The following year the parliament banned Solidarity, replacing it with a government-controlled trade union. Martial law officially ended in July 1983 but the government adopted new laws to restrict rights.

Solidarity rules
In 1989, after a series of strikes and demonstrations against the government's handling of the economy, Solidarity was offered the opportunity to take part in elections. Although a number of seats were reserved for Communists, Solidarity won every seat that they contested. In 1990, Lech Walesa, a former electrician in the Gdansk shipyard, was elected president.

POLAND AT A GLANCE
Area 120,727 square miles
Population 37,600,000
Capital Warsaw
Government Republic
Currency Zloty = 100 groszy
Language Polish
Religion Christian (95% Roman Catholic, 1% Polish Orthodox, 0.25% Lutheran)
Climate Continental; average temperature in Warsaw ranges from -5-0°C (23-32°F) in January to 15-24°C (59-75°F) in July
Main primary products Cereals, sugar beet, oilseed, potatoes, livestock, fish, timber; coal, sulphur, copper, zinc, lead, iron ore
Major industries Machinery, iron and steel, mining, chemicals, shipbuilding, food processing, agriculture, petroleum refining, fishing, forestry
Main exports Machinery, coal, foodstuffs, chemicals, non-ferrous metals, ships and boats, motor vehicles, clothing, iron and steel
Annual income per head (US$) 1800
Population growth (per thous/yr) 10
Life expectancy (yrs) Male 70 **Female** 75

Romania

A spirit of independence has long sustained the people of this much-invaded country. Unlike the peoples of other Balkan countries, the Romanians are not true Slavs. They claim to trace their descent directly back to the Romans who colonised their land; their language is Latinised, and Romania means 'the Roman land'.

Roman settlement: AD 106-271

The area corresponding to present-day Romania had a flourishing Bronze Age civilisation, which was destroyed by Scythian invaders from southern Russia c. 800 BC. The Scythians in turn were overrun by the Celtic Dacians, who migrated to Romania in the 3rd century BC. The Romans, under Trajan, conquered the area in AD 106, and it became one of the most prosperous parts of their empire. After the Roman withdrawal in 271, the country became the prey of barbarian invaders.

Conquest by Ottoman Turks

By the 13th century, two Christian principalities, Moldavia and Wallachia, had come into being. Though both were nominally independent, Wallachia was controlled by Hungarian Magyars, who had already annexed Transylvania, while Moldavia was a Polish satellite. Both states were subject to the Ottoman Turks by the 1500s.

Struggle for Independence

Centuries of Turkish oppression ended when, at the Congress of Paris held in 1856 to end the Crimean War, the principal European powers guaranteed the Romanians' right to elect their own rulers. In 1861, Moldavia and Wallachia were united to form Romania under the reforming prince Alexander Cuza.

First World War and after

Romania entered the First World War on the side of the Allies in 1916 – but was quickly defeated. Re-entering the war in 1918, it was rewarded at the peace conference by the restoration of Transylvania from Austro-Hungary and the acquisition of Bessarabia from Russia. Following the war, the Romanian government tried to carry out land and social reforms, but these attempts were defeated by the aristocracy. This failure, combined with the world-wide economic depression of the 1930s, drove Romanians in increasing numbers to either Communism or Fascism.

War on the side of Germany: 1941-4

Romania's king, Carol II, tried to keep his country neutral in the Second World War, but his prestige was ruined by successful territorial claims made against Romania by Hungary and Bulgaria – with German support – and Russia's re-occupation of the provinces of Bessarabia and North Bukovina in 1940. Later that year, Marshal Antonescu, the leader of the Romanian Fascist Party – the 'Iron Guard' – overthrew the king. In 1941, Romania joined in the German attack on Russia. But when the Eastern Front collapsed in 1944, Carol's successor, Michael, arrested Antonescu and declared war on Germany. Russian troops occupied the country.

Defiance of the USSR

In 1947 Michael was forced to abdicate and the country became a republic. Romania remained an obedient Soviet satellite until 1962 when the Romanians refused to give up their industrial programme, despite Russian demands that Romania should resume its designated role as agricultural 'reservoir' for the Soviet bloc. In 1971 President Nicolae Ceausescu stated that there should be no interference in the internal affairs of any national Communist Party. He had already condemned Russian intervention in Czechoslovakia and refused to join in attacking Chinese policy, retaining friendly ties with China despite the Chinese-Soviet rift. Romania recognised West Germany without consulting Moscow and was criticised for its part in arranging President Nixon's visit to China. In 1984, Romania again showed its independence by taking part in the Olympics in Los Angeles, boycotted by other Communist nations.

Revolution and after

Of all the East European rulers, Nicolae Ceausescu seemed the least vulnerable at the beginning of 1989. However, his rural resettlement programme had created enormous resentment among the Romanians and his desire to pay off Romania's debt to the West had reduced most of the people to abject poverty. The suppressed hatred boiled over in December 1989 when crowds turned out onto the streets to protest against the regime. On 22 December, the army refused to fire on a demonstration in central Bucharest and the troops turned against the regime. Ceausescu fled from Bucharest by helicopter, but was later arrested. He and his wife were executed on Christmas Day. The army joined opposition groups to form the National Salvation Front, which won a landslide victory in elections held the following year.

Bulgaria

The Slav country of Bulgaria, in the eastern Balkans, sprang into international prominence in the late 19th century, when the ruthless slaughter of Bulgarians by Turkish forces stirred the conscience of liberal Europe. Bulgaria was rescued by Russia, and the two countries remained closely linked for many years.

Slavs in Bulgaria
Slavic tribes first settled in Bulgaria c. AD 500, but a century later these Slavs were conquered by the Bulgars, a Turkic-speaking race from beyond the Danube, who gradually adopted the Slavs' language and culture. Bulgar independence – apart from a short period of Byzantine rule – lasted until the Ottoman conquest in 1396. The Bulgarians were the most oppressed subject people of the Ottoman Empire. Their suffering reached an extreme point in the suppression of Bulgarian nationalist movements during the 19th century, when thousands were massacred.

Congress of Berlin: 1878
Russia intervened in 1878 in support of the Bulgarians, whom they regarded as brother Slavs, and independence followed. But other powers became involved. Britain's prime minister, Benjamin Disraeli, did not want to see Russia grow too powerful, so he opposed the formation of a 'big Bulgaria', which he thought would become a natural ally of Russia. The south remained part of the Ottoman Empire, while the north, though still owing nominal allegiance to Turkey, was placed under the rule of a German prince, Alexander of Battenberg. In 1908, however, Ferdinand of Saxe-Coburg-Gotha, who had succeeded Alexander in 1887, took advantage of revolt in Constantinople to proclaim himself tsar of independent Bulgaria.

Wars and dictatorships: 1911-36
Under Ferdinand, Bulgaria became involved in war against Turkey, and against its Balkan neighbours, in 1911 and 1912.

In the First World War Bulgaria took the side of Germany. But the result was defeat, and in 1918 Ferdinand abdicated in favour of his son, Boris III.

After a few years of stability under the new tsar, there followed a decade of political confusion during which Macedonian terrorists tried to overthrow the Bulgarian regime. In 1936 a military dictatorship was established, and a year later Boris assumed supreme power.

Modern Bulgaria
Bulgaria again backed Germany in the Second World War, thereby gaining Greek and Romanian territory in 1940 and 1941. But Boris refused to declare war on the USSR, in view of the long ties of friendship between the two countries.

In 1944 the Bulgarians abandoned Germany and tried to make a separate peace with Britain and the USA – but the USSR took over the country. The monarchy was overthrown and the king went into exile; in 1946 a Communist 'people's republic' was set up, under Georgi Dimitrov.

After the Second World War, Bulgaria co-operated closely with the USSR. The nation's economic emphasis shifted from agriculture to industry – major industries are the production of chemicals and machinery, and food processing. Since 1980 the government has encouraged investment by allowing foreign companies to own up to 90 per cent of joint ventures. To make industry more effective, it was decided in 1982 that each enterprise must not pay out more in wages than its revenues after expenses.

In the autumn of 1989, as Communist regimes were being toppled in Eastern Europe, it seemed that the Bulgarian Communist Party would survive intact. But in November Todor Zhivkov, the General Secretary, was forced to resign. Opposition groups began to appear and demanded political pluralism. The Communists adopted a new name, the Bulgarian Socialist Party (but reaffirmed their allegiance to Marxism). Elections were held in June 1990, and to the astonishment of the West, most seats were won by the BSP.

BULGARIA AT A GLANCE
Area 42,823 square miles
Population 9,000,000
Capital Sofia
Government Republic
Currency Lev = 100 stotinki
Languages Bulgarian, Turkish
Religions Mainly atheist or non-religious; Christians include 25% Eastern Orthodox, 1% Roman Catholic; also 10% Muslim
Climate Continental in the mountains and north; Mediterranean in the south-facing valleys. Average temperature in Sofia ranges from -4-2°C (25-36°F) in January to 16-27°C (61-81°F) in July
Main primary products Wheat, barley, maize, grapes, sunflower seeds, apples, tobacco, cattle, sheep, timber; coal, lignite, oil and natural gas, manganese, uranium
Major industries Agriculture, tobacco processing, cement, iron and steel, coke, machinery, textiles, chemicals, fertilisers, leather goods, forestry, brewing and distilling, wine, oil and gas refining
Main exports Machinery, transport equipment, chemicals, cigarettes, meat, fruit, vegetables, tobacco, wines, spirits
Annual income per head (US$) 2900
Population growth (per thous/yr) 2
Life expectancy (yrs) Male 71 **Female** 76

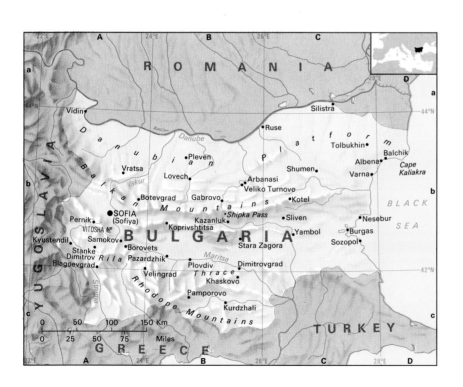

Picture Credits

p.9 M. Garanger; p.10 top Roy-Explorer; bottom Lehr-Diaf; p.11 M. Garanger; p.12 Schulthes-Rapho; p.13 top M. Garanger; bottom Mehta-Contact-Cosmos; p.14 Roy-Explorer; p.15 top Lehr-Diaf; bottom Roy-Explorer; p.16 Lehr-Diaf; p.16/17 Mehta-Cosmos-Contact; p.17 M. Garanger; p.18 M.Garanger; p.19 Mehta-Contact-Cosmos; p.20 M. Garanger; p.21 Roy-Explorer; p.22 Azenstarck-Bard-Rapho; p.23 Rowan-Ana; p.24 Carde-Explorer; p.25 top Lehr-Diaf; bottom J. Bottin; p.26 S. Held; p.26/7 Gohier-Diaf; p.27 C. Lénars; p.28 Azenstarck-Bard-Rapho; p.29 Robillard; p.30 Charlier-Ana; p.31 top Robillard; bottom Devaux-Lada; p.32 de Visser-Rapho; p.33 Cadre-Explorer; p.34 M. Garanger; p.35 M. Garanger; p.36 M. Garanger; p.37 top M. Garanger; bottom M. Garanger; p.38 C. Lénars. p.38/9 Garanger/Sipa Press; p.39 Mydons-Rapho; p.40 top M. Garanger; bottom M. Garanger; p.41 M. Garanger; p.42 M. Garanger; p.43 left M. Garanger; right M.-L. Maylin; p.44 Koch-Rapho; p.45 left Serraillier-Rapho; right S. Held; p.46 C. Lénars; p.47 M. Garanger; p.48 Roy-Explorer; p.49 A. Robillard; p.50 top Hawkes-Jacana; bottom Labat-Jacana; p.51 Varin-Jacana; p.52 Schultes-Rapho; p.53 Launois-Rapho; p.54 left M. Garanger; right Carde-Explorer; p.55 Obolensky-Ana; p.56 Gohier-Diaf; p.57 top Gohier-Diaf; bottom M. Garanger; p.58 M. Garanger; p.59 M. Garanger; p.60 C.Lénars; p.61 top Carde-Explorer; bottom M. Garanger; p.62 Koch-Rapho; p.63 left Koch-Rapho; right Schultes-Rapho; p.64 M. Garanger; p.65 M. Garanger; p.66 M. Garanger; p.66/7 M. Garanger; p.67 M. Garanger; p.68 Koch-Rapho; p.69 F.Jalain; p.70 top M. Garanger; bottom Sappa-Cedri; p.71 Sappa-Cedri; p.72 J.-M. Steinlein;

p.73 M. Garanger; p.74 top M. Garanger; bottom Sappa-Cedri; p.75 J.-M. Steinlein; p.76 top S. Bellows; bottom Sappa-Cedri; p.77 M. Garanger; p.78 G. Navarro; p.79 Harbutt-Cosmos; p.80 F. Jalain; p.81 F. Jalain; p.82 M. Garanger; p.83 left Erwitt-Magnum; right M. Garanger; p.84 F. Jalain; p.85 left F. Jalain; right Erwitt-Magnum; p.86 Sappa-Cedri; p.87 top J.-M. Steinlein; bottom M. Garanger; p.88 J.-M. Steinlein; p.89 Cappelle-Cedri; p.90 top A. Rona; bottom F. Peuriot; p.91 J. Bottin; p.92 F. Peuriot; p.93 top Goldman-Rapho; bottom Pasquier-Rapho; p.94/5 top P. Szapu; bottom Silvester-Rapho; p.95 J. Bonnefoy; p.96 P. Szapu; p.97 J. Bonnefoy; p.98 Welland-Rapho; p.99 P.Szapu; p.100 left Woodfin Camp-Cosmos; right F.Peuriot; p.101 P.Ploquin; p.102 F.Peuriot; p.103 left Lyon-Rapho; right C.Lénars; p.104 Goldman-Rapho; p.105 top Lyon-Rapho; bottom Cappelle-Cedri; p.106 J. Bottin; p.107 Woodfin Camp-Cosmos; p.108 Cappelle-Cedri; p.109 Barbey-Magnum; p.110 Sioen-Cedri; p.111 top Rousseau-Top; bottom Sioen-Cedri; p.112 Rousseau-Top; p.113 Sioen-Cedri; p.114 Barbey-Magnum; p.115 left J.-M. Steinlein; right Sioen-Cedri; p.116 Rousseau-Top; p.117 Sioen-Cedri; p.118 J.-M. Steinlein; p.119 left Sioen-Cedri; Barbey-Magnum; p.120 Sioen-Cedri; p.121 Sebert-Explorer; p.122 Vioujard-Gamma; p.123 top Guillou-Explorer; bottom Barbey-Magnum; p.124 left Sioen-Cedri; right Rousseau-Top; p.125 Rousseau-Top; p.126 top Sioen-Cedri; bottom Sioen-Cedri; p.127 Sioen-Cedri; p.128 Gamma; p.129 Weisbecker-Explorer; p.130 top P. Ploquin; bottom Sappa-Cedri; p.131 Marion-Valentine-Pix; p.132 Le Moine; p.133 top Weisbecker-Explorer; bottom Sappa-Cedri; p.134 P. Ploquin; p.135 Marion-Valentine-Pix; p.136 top Weisbecker-Explorer; bottom Weisbecker-Explorer;

p.137 Weisbecker-Explorer; p.138 M. Guillard-Scope; p.139 top Marion-Valentine-Pix; bottom Marion-Valentine Pix; p.140 Riboud-Magnum; p.141 C. Lénars; p.142 top Roy-Explorer; bottom J. Sebag; p.143 C. Lénars; p.144 J. Bottin; p.145 top J. Sebag; bottom Beuzen-Explorer; p.146 J. Bottin; p.147 Beuzen-Explorer; p.148 Holsnyder

Cover pictures:
Top: Robert Harding Picture Library
Bottom: Abbas-Magnum